Days Gone By

Sue Parrish

PBL Limited
Ottumwa Iowa

DAYS GONE BY

Copyright 2007 by Sue Parrish

Cover design copyright 2007 by Michael W. Lemberger

This edition published 2007

10 9 8 7 6 5 4 3 2 1

ISBN   1-892689-30-8
ISBN 13:   978-1-892689-30-6

Illustrations are used with permission. Photos from the collection of Michael W. Lemberger: back cover, pages 7, 8, 11, 15, 16, 26, 27, 28, 31, 33, 35, 36, 39, 54, 58, 59, 60, 64, 65, 66, 69, 70, 71, 79, 81, 83, 89, 91, 93, 94, 95, 98, 100, 101, 103, 104, 113, 117, 127, 129, 130. Photos by Michael W. Lemberger: pages 19, 21, 24, 25, 29, 40, 41, 43, 45, 47, 49, 50, 51, 53, 56, 57, 63, 85, 97, 123, 137. Photos from the collection of David Longdo: pages 72, 73, 75, 77, 87, 107, 108, 110, 111, 119, 133. Photos from the collection of Sue Parrish: front cover, back cover and pages 13, 23, 55, 109, 115, 120, 125, 140. Photo from the collection of Paul Anderson: page 135.

Printed in the United States of America

All rights reserved. Except for brief passages quoted in any review, the reproduction or utilization of this work in whole or in part, in any form or by any electronic, mechanical, or other means, now known or hereinafter invented, including xerography, photocopying and recording, or in any information storage and retrieval system, is forbidden without the express permission of the publisher. For permission contact:
  Rights Editor
  PBL Limited
  P.O. Box 935
  Ottumwa IA 52501-0935
  www.pbllimited.com

Copies of this book are available from PBL Limited. Visit our website at www.pbllimited.com, or see page 142 for details on how to order by mail.

To my husband,
Richard Lawrence Parrish, 1942-2003,
"Always United"

and
Pat Myers-Lock,
who helped me through the worst of times.
Thank you.

I wish to acknowledge Michael and LeAnn Lemberger; Pat Myers-Lock, Rusty Corder and the Wapello County Historical Society; the Wapello County Genealogical Society; Mary Ann Lemon and the Ottumwa Public Library; The Courier's editor, Judy Krieger and publisher, Tom Hawley; Molly Myers Naumann; Mr. and Mrs. Harvey Grooms, Thomas Quinn, David Longdo, Paul Anderson, and last but not least, Terry Gipson, my computer guru.

This is not a scholarly work, nor is it intended to be. It is a work of historic anecdotes gleaned from the archives, newspapers, and history books housed in the library of the Wapello County Historical Museum and the Wapello County Genealogical Library, as well as the Ottumwa Public Library. This was compiled to challenge you to relax, close your eyes, allow your imagination to drift, and become a part of the days gone by.

-- Sue Parrish

O the days gone by! O the days gone by!
The apples in the orchard, and the pathway through
The rye:
The chirping of the robins, and the whistle of the quail
As he piped across the meadows sweet
as any nightingale:
When the bloom was on the clover, and the blue was
in the sky.
And my happy heart brimmed over—in the days gone by!

--James Whitcomb Riley

Cover illustration: C B & Q Railroad conductor and Civil War veteran Daniel B. Cowles mows the lawn while his sons Joe and Bert cavort on their bicycle. Parrish collection.

Table of Contents

Into Oblivion 6
Eminent Domain 8
Roots, Wolves, and a Greyhound 10
The Virgin Prairie 12
A Great Legacy 14
Wolves, Mosquitoes, and
    Log Cabins 16
1851 Hidden Home 18
Hard Work: The Tie that Binds 20
A Woman of Superior Intelligence
    and Firm Convictions 22
Codes of Honor 24
Justice in Ormanville 26
Territories on the West 28
From One Side to Another 30
"Went Raven Mad" 32
Great American Hog Drives 34
Pick the Moniker 36
Cabin Among the Trees 38
A Bed and Breakfast 40
Call to Arms 42
On the Tennessee River 44
Tales From Vicksburg 46
April Memories 48
"Kiss My Sweet Little Boys for Me" 50
Bravery Knows No Color 52
Anecdotes and Petticoats 54
Dead Men Meet 56
General James Shields and Molly 58
Bittersweet Victory 60
Jarrett Garner's Memories 62
In Spite of Jack Frost 64
Men and Their Vehicles 66
Caster's Flats 68
Cigars, Bicycles and Cameras 70
Little Lady from Genoa 72
The Great Aphrodisiac 74

The Staff of Life 76
The Egg Lady 78
Crates and Candy 80
Proprietress of Dry Goods 82
Blake's Sister Mary 84
The Art of Entertaining 86
The Village on the Other Side 88
Village Challenges 90
Impeded Village Growth 92
South Ottumwa: Another Side
    of the Story 94
South Ottumwa's Gold Rush 96
Latter-Day Noah's Ark 98
Father Ward's Call 100
Mr. Diehn and His Boxes 102
Edith's Room 104
The Invisible Working Women 106
"A Brilliant Society Event" 108
A Work for Carrie Nation 110
Son of Zeus 112
A Fateful February Fifth 114
In Celebration of
    Independence Day 116
The North Green Home 118
Civic Leaders' Duplex 120
Nickels and Dimes 122
English Tudor Years 124
12,618 Panes of Glass 126
The Evil Within 128
The Days of Thanksgiving 130
Monday Mornings 132
Swoosh and Soot 134
An Ignoble End 136
Epilogue 138
Bibliography 139
About the Author 141

INTO OBLIVION

When the Sauk and Fox tribes signed the treaty with the whites on October 11, 1842, Fox Chief Wapello had been dead for almost exactly seven months, having passed away the previous March 15. Preferring to hunt on old hunting grounds along the Skunk River where wild game abounded, with the inducement of wild honey, Wapello and his band would leave the Des Moines River area frequently and travel north to the Skunk, as he did during the last few days of his life.

Some accounts have him dying of pneumonia contracted from falling asleep in the rain after a bout of drinking. It is reported that he didn't drink to the extent of Keokuk, but limited it to "sprees." One account states that he began these in 1836, when he traded his horse for a barrel of whiskey and "invited his friends to help him drown his sorrow" after a favorite son of his had been killed. Whatever the cause of his death, the 55-year-old chief became suddenly ill, lingering only a few days and dying on the banks of Rock Creek in Jackson Township, Keokuk County, where he had pitched a lodge. Keokuk County resident Samuel Hardesty brought his body back to the Indian Agency (the present-day city of Agency) by ox cart the same day, being accompanied by 22 braves and three women.

It is little wonder that the Indians strayed from their villages along the banks of the Des Moines and away from the Agency. Their villages were described in 1844 by the Congregational minister and missionary, Rev. Benjamin Spaulding, as "rather the haunts of beasts than the abodes of men. Not a tree, nor shrub, a garden, nor a well, nor the slightest mark of beauty or comfort, was anywhere to be seen, even the wild grass had been beaten by continual tramping, till not a blade nor root was left, and as the savages were away on a hunting expedition, the stillness of death reigned over their desolate homes." He continues, "These are to be removed in less than a year, to a region beyond the Missouri River. If, by this removal, they were placed forever beyond reach of whiskey smugglers and other vicious white men, it would be a blessing to them instead of a curse."

With the signing of the 1842 treaty ceding their ground, the Sauk and Fox were to be gone by the end of October, 1845. It was not unusual for the earliest settlers to view the sad departure of these Native Americans, as well as having them silently appear at their door begging for food, as happened at a cabin which was located in the area of Ottumwa later known as Central Addition. One Indian lost a finger as he tried to enter the cabin of the George Gillaspy family by pulling the leather string on the door. In fear, because her husband was away at the mill, Mrs. Gillaspy took a hatchet to the intruder. Not uttering a sound, the Indian left, minus a finger.

Lemberger collection

Chief Wapello's gravesite, about 1930

Benjamin Spaulding also reflected upon their leaving: "The eager strife of the whites to gain possession of the country just left by the Indians, bears a most striking contrast to the slow and reluctant step of the recent owners in leaving their native groves and prairies, and all of the scenery associated with past joys for a distant, unknown and undesired country. Many of them were seen in companies of twenties or perhaps fifties, floating in their light canoes, down the swift current of the Des Moines, as if the stream of time were hurrying them into the gulf of oblivion, and yet they could not fail to stop awhile in this well-remembered spot to take a few more fish, or to go ashore and pass the night in some old grove which had often sheltered them, and was still more hospitable and grateful to them than the dwellings of their pale-faced supplanters; or to linger awhile about some place consecrated by the ashes of departed friends, and then pass on to look upon it again no more forever."

It was the pioneers near the Iowa River who helped members of the Fox chief Poweshiek's band stay along the Iowa River, as they trickled back from Kansas, homesick for their former hunting grounds. By 1857 there were eight wickiups on the Iowa River and four on the Cedar. This was the beginning of the Tama Settlement, which the Fox were able to eventually purchase with their annuities.

Days Gone By

EMINENT DOMAIN

It is not unusual for obscure footnotes in history to be overlooked for years, and one such footnote occurs with licensed Indian fur trader John Sanford, whose fort was located just below the mouth of Sugar Creek.

When Captain James Allen of the 1st Dragoons, a West Point classmate of Robert E. Lee, was sent to this area to protect the rights of the Indians from the white squatters for the seven months prior to the area being opened for settlement May 1, 1843, he chose the site of the trading post operated by John Sanford. Sanford had been a clerk in St. Louis for William Clark of the famous exploration team of Lewis and Clark, and in 1853 he was legally recognized as the owner of the slave Dred Scott,

Lemberger collection

Horse Thief Cave, Garrison Rock, Wapello County -- taken before 1899

his wife and two children. Though the events surrounding Dred Scott are well known, the association with him of John Sanford, a licensed fur trader here, is not.

Dred Scott brought suit against Sanford in what became the landmark Supreme Court case of Dred Scott vs. Sanford. Scott sued on the premise that he was a free man and citizen due to the Missouri Compromise of 1820 which barred slavery from the lands acquired by the Louisiana Purchase that were north of the 36' 30" latitude. However, the Supreme Court ruled the Missouri Compromise was unconstitutional and the slaves were not citizens of the United States, therefore denying Scott freedom. This is considered one of the worst, if not *the* worst, decision ever to come down from the Supreme Court. The freedom of Dred Scott and his family was purchased May 26, 1857 by the sons of his first owner, Peter Blow. Scott died of tuberculosis September 17, 1858.

Contrary to popular belief, the fort was not located on what became known as Garrison Rock; Sanford's trading post was a cluster of log buildings just below the mouth of Sugar Creek approximately 1/8 mile east of the Garrison Rock caves. Squatters had dug in their heels in the caves to hide before the area was opened, allowing them a distinct advantage over those who legally awaited the firing of the gun at midnight April 30, 1843. The dragoons did not bother these squatters unless they left the caves to make a claim. The garrison cemetery was located on Garrison Rock for the interment of those soldiers who died during the seven months the dragoons were stationed there. The remains of some civilians also rest in that cemetery.

Captain Allen named the site of his short term post Fort Sanford in honor of the fur trader, and when he left, the log buildings allowed shelter for the family of Elias Kitterman, among others, while these settlers searched for new lands to claim. The Kittermans settled in Dahlonega Township where Elias and his brother, Peter, opened a blacksmith shop.

Captain Allen founded Fort Des Moines after leaving Fort Sanford, and in the summer of 1844 he and his dragoons traveled 740 miles in search of the source of the Des Moines River while exploring what is now southwest Minnesota and northwest Iowa.

As a lieutenant colonel, Allen enlisted and took command of 500 Mormon men in Council Bluffs in July, 1846 to facilitate their westward migration and to provide reserve forces in the Mexican War. However, James Allen died suddenly August 23, 1846 at Ft. Leavenworth and is buried at Ft. Leavenworth National Cemetery. Capt. Jefferson Hunt was ordered to take command of what was called the Mormon Battalion, and he led the way to Santa Fe.

Days Gone By

ROOTS, WOLVES, and A GREYHOUND

A great many of the pioneers crossed the Mississippi by raft to Keokuk bringing with them their sheep, cattle and what goods their wagons could carry, and headed northwest to what they called "The New Purchase." As families and friends often came together, they would locate a campsite and strike out from there. Reaching this goal, it was then time to find unclaimed ground they could call their own, which usually amounted to a quarter of a section (one hundred sixty acres).

Once the farmer's claim was made, the first order of business was a shelter, which for many consisted of a shed with slough grass used for a roof. Others began immediately to build a house of round logs with a puncheon floor while living in their wagons. Then would follow hewed log houses with board floors and shingled roofs with the shingles being made of "clapboards split from logs. They were about eight inches wide and held in place on the roof by means of a log laid in rows like shingles. There were no nails."

After the log house came a brick home for many, with those built in the 1850s still dotting the countryside as late as forty years ago. Alas, though they were considered quite a home when built, they were very primitive by modern standards. Though two stories high, and sitting on a basement, the average brick farm house consisted of three small rooms on the main floor and two or three smaller rooms above. They were cold and clammy in the winter and damp in the summer. Many a *Hallelujah!* was raised with great rejoicing when these once Grand Dames of the prairie fell to the farmer's wrecking ball and were replaced with a modern 20th century dwelling!

The prairie was covered with bluestem grass and resin weed from six to ten feet high, which was the home of rabbits too numerous to count, wolves, prairie chickens and quail. The prairie chickens nested in the grass in the spring and summer. The wolves would come near the homes on the prairie during the night, setting hairs on end with their howls. Abraham Stevens of Highland Township had a greyhound whose waking hours were spent chasing wolves, as his stamina allowed, frequently before breakfast, and bringing one home on many occasions. Sheep especially had to be closely guarded and confined at night from these predators. Their wool was needed to make sheets, blankets, clothing and other household goods, as there were no merchants nearby in those first lean years.

Life on the prairie was not for the faint-hearted. With everything done by hand with the crudest of implements, it took everyone who was able working to survive. Shirkers and loafers were ostracized. It took as many as six or more oxen to turn over the prairie sod for the first time, as the tough grasses, matted several feet deep where there had not been a recent prairie fire, had roots unwilling to give up without a fight, snapping and groaning beneath the plow.

Competine, a minor chief, was one of the last Indians seen leaving: He was riding a horse with the snapping of the roots — his roots — ringing in his ears, as his eleven wives followed on foot.

Lemberger collection

Log cabin in Wapello County, taken before 1899. At the time the photograph was taken, the cabin was still being used as a home.

Days Gone By

THE VIRGIN PRAIRIE

When the cool evenings of September arrive, and the corn begins to turn, the imagination is carried back to days gone by captured only through the vision of others who lived those days. Their written memories of what was before them when they first set foot on this virgin prairie with the bright blue cloudless sky meeting the ten foot high grasses — matted and tangled with the centuries, disturbed only by prairie fires — leave us to wonder at the sights, smells and sounds of those days teaming with wildlife, now long extinct in this area.

By the time this area was opened for settlement in 1843, a blacksmith in Illinois had already invented the most valuable tool for the taming of the matted, tangled prairie which would become known as the "bread basket of the world." John Deere's plow, invented in 1837, was a godsend to the pioneer farmers. The steel blade was sharp enough to cut through the grasses while smooth enough to throw off mud. He had invented the invaluable "Sodbuster" which opened the prairie.

William Henry Stevens (1844-1919) came with his parents and extended family to Highland Township in 1848, camping on the banks of the Big Cedar Creek, the site which is now the McCormick Cemetery. Though the area had been open for five years, there were no houses on the prairie, as the family were some of the first settlers in this township. He left us with detailed written memories of the life and culture of those pioneer years:

"There were houses and fences to build and there was no small amount of labor attached to making the rails and getting them in the ground in order to fence in even a small farm. Then there was the sod to break, and it took a good strong team to turn the first sod. Then crops to plant and cultivate. Everything was done by hand. When I look back over my boyhood days, I shudder at the problems they were up against, feeding and clothing us and keeping us together; but they did it and were always clear of debt. We had plenty for ourselves and always had something to spare to a neighbor in distress, the result of good management and close attention to business."

Though there were several religious denominations represented in the neighborhood, the Stevens family were Primitive Baptists, and in the beginning, all

Sue Parrish

Lemberger collection

Alpine Log Church. This building dates from a much later period. Early in the area's settlement, church services were held in homes.

denominations joined together and held services in the Stevens home. Later, the Stevens family held services for their denomination once a month with members attending from all over the county and spending two days in the Stevens home. William Stevens remembers,

"I always looked forward to these meetings with a great deal of pleasure. To me, it was like being visited by relatives. My parents, too, were always pleased to have a crowd. They never seemed to mind the trouble or expense of feeding so many, they would say, "Pshaw! We never miss it." It came perfectly natural for the visiting women to lay right hold and help prepare the meals, talking and laughing, and visiting all the time. I really believe they came as near observing the admonition 'Love one another' as it is possible for a community of people to do."

Everyone looked forward to these monthly meetings with anticipation, because they were the primary source for socialization in those early days, since the church was the center of the pioneers' social lives. They were especially important to those who had moved farther west leaving beloved family members behind.

Days Gone By

A GREAT LEGACY

A child of the prairie, born in 1844 in McDonough County, Illinois to Abraham and Catherine Stevens, and growing up on a farm in Highland Township, William Henry Stevens left his family with a written memory of those pioneer farm years in Wapello County. These "Recollections," written before his death in 1919, are a vivid, spell-binding account of those who came before us and set down their roots, which became our roots. The following, taken from his recollections, exemplifies one of their greatest legacies:

"When I was about five years old, the men in the neighborhood built a log schoolhouse about forty rods from our house. It was built like all of the other houses in the country at that time, round logs with a clapboard roof and a big fireplace. All of the houses had fireplaces. I think Grandfather Stevens had the first stove I ever saw. There was a log left out on one side of the schoolhouse about three feet above the floor. Wooden pins were put in the log below and a board laid on them for a writing desk. The scholars would take turns standing there practicing their writing lessons. Glass was set in a crude frame filling the space where the log was out, and this constituted the only window in the house. For seats we had small logs split and turned flat side up with wooden pins in them for legs. They were usually about ten feet long and would seat six small scholars. There were no desks. James Davis was my first teacher and the first one that taught at that house. The other teachers as I remember were Henry Palmer, D. P. Williams, Charlie Legget and Seth Sampson. I suppose that each one of them boxed my ears at different times on general principles, if for no other reason, as these were days of the Hoosier Schoolmaster when 'Licking and Learning' went together. And it seemed to be the opinion of the teachers, at least, that it is necessary to lick a boy about so often just to keep his mind from wandering. But the only real thrashing I ever got at school was given me by Seth Sampson, and I always thought it was undeserved. It was this way: I was sitting on a seat between John Gray and Hez McCormick, all of our books held up in front of our faces pretending to be reading. Sampson was pretty even tempered, but this was his day off. He had just notified us that there had been entirely too much whispering. Hez, without moving the book that was in front of him, said in a whisper, "John, where does the first fly come from in the spring?" Sampson drew a hickory switch down from over the window and gave the three of us a good sound thrashing."

Recalling the original pioneers, Stevens states, "The old settlers, as I remember them, have all passed over. Among them were James West; James, Guy, and Robert Gray; George Godfrey; Guilford Davis; Minor Kirkpatrick; Seth Sampson; Jesse Buckner; the Kittermans; Caswell Dennis, Robert and William McCormick; Benjamin B. Stevens; and my father, Abraham V. Stevens."

Most pioneers were buried within the community they founded, and so it happened with those who claimed new homes near the Big Cedar Creek, the site of what is now McCormick Cemetery.

The first Highland Township schoolhouse was thought to have been constructed on ground donated by John Guy Gray.

Parrish collection

John Guy Gray (right) and grandson Elliot Gray

WOLVES, MOSQUITOES and LOG CABINS

There were many wild beasts afoot in the early days of settlement, including the large, black timber wolf and the smaller gray wolf, who prowled the prairies – making it impossible for the early settlers to raise sheep and other small livestock. During winter months, these predators came closer and closer to inhabited human settlements, allowing for large wolf hunts which in those early years yielded hundreds of wolf pelts. The hunts were not limited to only winter months, but what a terrifying chorus must have been heard across the prairie with the howling of wolves joined by the howls of canines of the domesticated kind used to hunt this predator!

Lemberger collection

Though the exact location is not known, this double log cabin is thought to have been located near Ottumwa, in Wapello County. It may have been the first double log cabin built in the county.

Sue Parrish

The wolves were not the only "wild beasts" to be contended with. Insects of the mosquito and fly kind tormented the pioneers unmercifully. Settlers told of the days "too terrible to dwell on" due to mosquito bites and the hoards of flies. The days before Tanglefoot, the "non poisonous fly destroyer" and DDT, the poisonous destroyer, were nearly unbearable. Both sides of the river were inundated with flies and mosquitoes, with the area near the river a swamp and marshland.

As there were no screened doors or windows, people escaped to the loft if they were lucky enough that their cabin had one. On the north side of the Des Moines River, the loft of the log tavern served the purpose. The flies were so numerous that in order to eat, a limb filled with leaves had to be in perpetual motion over the food during mealtime, while smudge pots were kept going night and day to drive away the mosquitoes.

If that wasn't enough to contend with, being near and on the river, there were always snakes. These settlers could be grateful in one respect: As they were living in cabins and not sod huts, the snakes would not, as an ordinary occurrence, come dropping from the ceiling as they did in the "soddies" of Nebraska and the Dakotas—truly plains states with little woodlands. Praise the Almighty for woods and cabins!

Upon arriving from Ohio in 1854, an early pioneer woman describing the area of what was to become Chester Avenue in south Ottumwa, conjures up a log cabin nestled among the trees, nearly as described in *The Little House in the Big Woods* by Laura Ingalls Wilder. The woman writes, "It was all woods then, with a little road running through. I didn't think then that there would be anything over here."

She goes on to state that Ottumwa was "the funniest little place" she had ever seen. The pioneer continues with her early experiences, relating that farm families would sell blackberries to townspeople. The women and children would go ahead to sell the berries while the men followed behind in an ox-drawn wagon to deliver them. There was only one problem: "There weren't many houses to visit." She recalls that if you traded at the store near the bridge, which was also the first store in South Ottumwa, you could cross the toll bridge to the north side free.

Another pioneer who arrived in 1854 from Ohio lived for a while in a log cabin owned by Mr. Inskeep before a home was built on the 200 acres her father had purchased to farm on the south side. She remembers only two houses there, with one being the ferry house.

1851 HIDDEN HOME

In 1843 the first log cabin was built on the banks of the Des Moines River in the western part of Center Township by Paris Caldwell, when he claimed one hundred and twenty acres of wilderness to turn into a farm. In 1851 high water forced him to move and build his home on higher ground on a bluff overlooking the river. This home, a much larger cabin than the original one, still stands at 1501 West Second Street, though it is hidden, encased within later construction. Viewing the structure today, it is not hard to imagine a cabin within, as the home standing now reveals a style from long ago. Sixty acres of the original one hundred and twenty were incorporated into the city limits and had been platted by the time of Caldwell's death in 1899. It is known as Caldwell's First Addition.

When Paris Caldwell first set foot on his new farm, the Indians were still here going up and down the river to Eddyville, where there was a trading post. Caldwell himself knew all of the local chiefs, and traded and bartered with them until they left in 1845. As the river was also one mode of transportation for the whites, both Indians and whites must have glided past each other numerous times on what was then a crystal-clear waterway.

Mr. Caldwell cleared his land while becoming a prominent citizen. He married Margaret Hackney two years after settling here, and the couple had a family of eight children at the time of Margaret's death in 1863. He soon remarried, and his second wife, the widow of William Walker, had one child, before her death in 1877 left Caldwell a widower for a second time, at age fifty-nine. He did not marry again.

Paris Caldwell was born in Virginia March 13, 1818; his father was a native of Scotland. Paris came to Iowa at age twenty-three in 1841, staying in Burlington for a short time before moving on to what became Davis County, where he stayed until this area was opened for settlement and he could claim his one hundred and twenty acres. It was reported in his obituary in *The Courier* of April 6, 1899, that it was on his farm that the tree stood, under which the Indians and the government agreed on the treaty which opened up this area for settlement. The obituary goes on to tell us that the tree, still standing at the time of Caldwell's death, gave Caldwell "great pride in caring for it."

Mr. Caldwell belonged to the fraternal order of the Masons, as did many others in his day.

Michael W. Lemberger

Paris Caldwell's original log cabin is said to be enclosed within the walls of this house at 1501 West Second Street, shown in 2007.

Members of his lodge served as pallbearers as he was buried from the West End Presbyterian Church. His remains were interred in Ottumwa Cemetery with Masonic rites, April 7, 1899, two days after his death. Four of his nine children preceded him in death.

The encased cabin at 1501 West Second Street is fittingly situated between Caldwell Street on the east and Paris Street on the southwest. The street names are a reminder of the first settler in this part of Ottumwa, who had the good fortune to have his property considered prime real estate at the time of his death over one hundred years ago.

HARD WORK: THE TIE THAT BINDS

The pioneer wife and mother left the comfort of the known for the unknown. Though many left nothing behind but poverty, many came unwillingly, carrying in their hearts the loved ones and friends most would never see again.

Many young couples who had been recently married, like Mary and Lewis Rupe, set out in 1845 for the vast unknown with parents or other friends and relatives. A first child was often born on the way from Ohio, Indiana or other points east, or born within the first year of striking a claim. These children came into the world to the most rudimentary of log homes or the backs of wagons.

Mary Rupe was to be one of the most fortunate of mothers, as all of her seven children survived into adulthood. Not so for nearly everyone else. Reverend Benjamin Spaulding, who founded the first church in Ottumwa — the First Congregational Church — and four others in surrounding communities, lamented in a letter to his superiors in Massachusetts, "About four weeks since, death entered our dwelling for the third time and bereaved us of our only remaining child. A single day passed and we were called again to follow to the grave, a niece, a sweet little girl...."

These women were responsible for making the supply of clothing by weaving sheets, coverlets and cloth as they cooked; planted and cared for a garden; preserved food goods; laundered; knitted socks, shawls, sweaters, caps and mittens, and sewed clothing by hand for the family from the fabric they had woven. There was candle making and soap making. Making soap was a very disagreeable task, a back-breaking, all-day affair which took place in the fall after the first frost, when butchering had taken place and fat was available. The making of lye soap was not only labor intensive, due to the constant stirring over an outdoor fire, but the odor of the lye and fat as it bubbled together was very disagreeable. A year's supply of soap was usually made during this one-day marathon event most dreaded by all.

These mothers cared for the sick and prepared bodies for burial. They were pregnant nearly every one of their child-bearing years, and frequently, with a newborn, were placed under the sod. They would be prepared for burial by the closest relative or neighbor.

One Wapello County pioneer who came as a child in 1843 recalled, "We thought we were having the best time in the world then, but I see now that we had pretty bad

Photo by Michael W. Lemberger

Candle molds -- used by the pioneer wife and mother to make the family's lights.
From the personal collection of author Sue Parrish.

times." When families ran out of meal and flour, neighbors would share, and those who returned from a mill would supply those who had none. "We always paid back what we borrowed." Even the bark mill at the tannery in Dahlonega was "pressed into service for grinding grain" during emergencies.

Another, who came as a child in 1848, remembering those years stated, "It would be impossible for me to record the hardships encountered by the pioneers of this country... there was no small amount of labor attached to making the rails and getting them in the ground in order to fence in even a small farm. Everyone who was large enough had to work and work hard."

Days Gone By

A WOMAN OF SUPERIOR INTELLIGENCE and FIRM CONVICTIONS

A memory related by an elderly woman as reported in a 1923 edition of the *Ottumwa Daily Courier* gives a vivid impression of a particular pioneer woman as seen through the eyes of a child. Though the name of this pioneer is long forgotten, she surely typifies our idea of what the pioneer woman was.

"She always came to our house in the spring. As a child I reasoned it out that she had learned that the wild mustard, young lambs-quarters and tender plantain made their first appearance in that vicinity. The morning after her arrival she would go out with pan and knife and gather the choicest of the early plants. She seemed not to have to hunt for the best, always walking straight and direct to them. Sourdock and a few horseradish leaves were added, a hog's jowl was cooked with them, and for that dinner she made her special corn bread of yellow meal mixed only with water and a little salt, baking it on a hot pan over the coals."

From what point east the pioneer woman had traveled into Wapello County was not known, but in those days it did not matter. She wore an "ample apron" tied securely around the waist of her erect figure over her dress made of homespun. It is noted that she wore a tight-fitting cap on her head with a "small frill and scant ties." The simplicity of her cap accentuated her pecuniary prudence.

The evenings were spent in candle light around an open fire with lively discussions, "always on the unsettled question of the plan of salvation as laid down in the Bible." This was not unusual, as religion was one of the main topics of conversation in those days. However, political discussions were also at the top of the list. When this particular woman visited, the discussion surrounding salvation was evidently never settled. One of the participants in the discussion believed in predestination and

Rachel Elliot Gray, photographed with her Bible

foreordination while another was "not so sure of points in the doctrine; each proving his or her assertion with quotations from the scripture until the argument became as sharp and decisive as the click of knitting needles." This woman was a "woman of superior intelligence and firm convictions."

The adults always enjoyed her visits and "honored and respected her," but though she never reprimanded a child, she also showed no special interest in them and it was made evident to children that they were to "be seen and not heard." This probably explains why as an adult, this child could not remember the woman's name, where she lived or anything else about her. But we receive a picture of a no-nonsense, intelligent woman who was able to meet any adversity with the strength and determination of character grounded in strong religious faith.

Days Gone By

CODES OF HONOR

In our early years, this was the West – and when thinking of events of claim jumpers and cattle rustlers, as depicted in the western movies and television series which prevailed in the 1950s and into the 1960s, we do not think of this happening in our historic past. But it did, and justice usually prevailed, one way or the other.

There were many unwritten codes of honor in those days, and bidding on another's claim at a land sale was one. An instance of this, resulting in a man being tried for murder, took place on the south side of the Des Moines River. A gentleman by the name of Dr. Wright learned a fatal lesson when he bid on a claim taken by a man named Captain Ross. A gunfight between Captain Ross and Dr. Wright immediately ensued, leaving Captain Ross with a serious wound to the face, and Dr. Wright dead. Though Ross was tried for murder, he was acquitted.

Then James Woody of Dahlonega jumped a claim and sold it for $200. This resulted in one man falling dead after being hit in the head by a rock. The marshal from Fairfield was sent for, but the inhabitants of Dahlonega, having frontier justice on their side, more than strongly encouraged the marshal to return to Fairfield, which he did with great haste.

The men of Dahlonega made things very uncomfortable for Woody, who was a storekeeper and the son of Revolutionary War veteran Jonathan R. Woody, who is buried in Dahlonega Cemetery. In one instance a hole was bored into a keg of whiskey through a crack in the logs of James Woody's store, and the whiskey was siphoned off, emptying the keg, with the whiskey being offered free of charge to those who needed their thirst quenched. However, the culprits were never identified.

Michael W. Lemberger

Sue Parrish

Woody, in turn, also being the justice of the peace, had a number of individuals whom he suspected of the dastardly deed arrested for working and swearing on Sunday. When the day of the trial came, many inhabitants were in attendance, coming from far and wide. One, James Richards, came into the courtroom carrying a large quantity of hickory switches. This prompted Woody's son, Jack, to dash into the courtroom for a quick conference with his father. Woody, deciding it would be uncomfortable to be whipped with hickory switches, announced that news had come which made it necessary to dismiss court and resume the cases later. Again frontier justice prevailed and the cases were never heard of again.

There was more than one incident of claim jumping, and suffice to say they did not always end in violence; some were inadvertent, with these being settled amicably.

Cheating at cards was another event that could be dangerous to one's health. Samuel Dorr, in section 34 of Highland Township, had a number of farmhands in a barn gambling at cards while drinking. A heated argument ensued, leaving one card player with a gunshot wound. Family tradition recalls from that day forward, Mr. Dorr did not allow card playing or gambling by his farm hands.

There are many incidents, recorded and unrecorded, such as those above, but settling in the wilderness was not for the faint of heart. Settlers kept order and meted justice in the best way they could for all concerned.

Gravesite of Jonathan Woody, Dahlonega Cemetery

Michael W. Lemberger

Days Gone By

JUSTICE IN ORMANVILLE

From time immemorial the acquisition of land and property has dwelt in the heart of man. It is never ending and will only be stopped by the proverbial "Second Coming." An account of "land grabbing" and how it was settled in Green Township by those pioneers whose names are synonymous with the settlement of Ormanville, is related in the April 4, 1851 issue of *The Courier*.

The story relates how the residents of that township met at the home of Benjamin Baum to decide what should be done concerning the issue of George W. Kendrick for entering Gabriel Higdon's claim. By 1851 tempers were not as hot as they had been in 1843 over claim infringements, so the thought of doing personal bodily harm to the perpetrator, if uttered, was not recorded. Other means were taken under advisement with a committee of three, including Benjamin Baum, Joseph Glover and Benjamin Reed, approaching Kendrick and offering him $52.50 for the property, which he refused. The committee then opted for a compromise offering him $26.25 for half of it. This he also refused and according to him, he "would die first" before he gave it up. His parents agreed with him, as did other relatives by the name of Hart. With this, Kendrick's final pronouncement, the township residents passed the following resolution:

Lemberger collection

Lemberger collection

"Resolved—That we will disown the Kendrick family and the Hart family as neighbors until the said Kendrick comes forward and makes a compromise with the said Higdon for said land.

"Resolved— That the proceedings of the meeting be published in the DES MOINES REPUBLIC AND COURIER."

The resolutions were signed by Benjamin Baum, J. H. Glover, David Shewey, John Benson, John Benson, Jr., A. J. Smart, Jonathan Heckart, Paul Shepherd, Hiram Frederick, Henry Knowles, Benjamin Reed, William Knight, George Coughron, A. N. Rush, W. Kennady, H. S. Thompson, R. S. Rush, Hiram Chase, Joseph Higdon, W. H. Rush, N. Rush, Elwood Hammit, L. B. Wilkinson, R. Jackson, Moses Hale and Greenville Hale.

What was the outcome? Well, we do know that Kendrick was not shot between the eyes, strung-up on the nearest tree by a rope or tarred and feathered, as some perpetrators of this crime were subjected to, but according to historian Sylvano A. Wueschner in his Book *Ormanville*, the Kendrick and Hart families had disappeared from Green Township by 1860.

So was the way of the west.

TERRITORIES ON THE WEST

It was always a very welcome relief for those having moved west to receive a letter from home, while those left behind were very eager to learn of the new life on the frontier. Such was the case with Walter P. Rowell, who had traveled with his wife Maria to Wapello County from New Hampshire, and responded to a letter dated July 2nd, 1854 with a letter from Ottumwa dated July 30th, 1854 to "Dear Brother and Sister."

Mr. Rowell was very optimistic for the future here, as the prospect of the railroad had increased the price of property and had drastically increased business. Mr. Rowell's profession is unknown, but his letter to those back home stated that he and his partner, Mr. Harlan, had all of the business they could handle. He was also optimistic for river improvements. The health of everyone was also on his mind and he was glad to learn that his family in New Hampshire was in good health. Reporting on his family, he stated: "We have been much more favored than formerly; my health has been pretty good without even a symptom of the ague. Maria has not been as stout as usual, but she has done her work."

Given the cultural status of the day, the family in the east no doubt was able to read between the lines and understood Maria's health problems very well indeed. The Rowells had lost ten-month-old Amelia Ann the previous August, with Maria pregnant to give birth to Walter H. in February, and he was not in good health at the time the letter was written.

Rowell answers an inquiry concerning the western territories with, "You wished to know something of our new territories on the west. I can hardly give an opinion owing to the various and contradictory reports which we get here within two hundred miles of its boundary. There is an article in the New York Weekly Tribune of the 1st of July that comes nearer to the summed up statements than anything I could write; that is Nebraska (admitted to the Union in 1867) is of but little account except for a small strip along the Missouri River, while Kansas (admitted to the Union in 1861) is a tolerable country." He continues, "A citizen of our country has lately returned from a trip to Kansas. He says it is the finest country he ever saw for 80 miles up the Kansas River; he is an old Kentuckian, and anti-slavery man, says there is some slaves in there, but thinks the free people will soon out number them."

Politics was much on the minds of men and was the foremost subject discussed. Walter tells of his opinion of Senator Stephen A. Douglas, in part, "You think Douglas got up his bill through selfishness. (The Kansas-Nebraska Act, which Douglas sponsored, repealed the Missouri Compromise of 1820.) I do not think so. I believe he was pure and honest in his motives as ever he was in doing any act of his life. And to say that it was all through selfishness, is to say but little for the balance of Congress."

Historians may have a different assessment of the Little Giant from Illinois than Mr. Rowell, as Douglas had his eye on the presidency, which he lost to Abraham Lincoln. Time has proven that the motives of congressmen have remained much the same.

Wapello County was not kind to Walter and Maria Rowell, as not all had their dreams come true. Their hopes for the future were dashed with the death of their son, Albert, who died May 23, 1858 at the age of eight years. The Rowells disappeared from Ottumwa's history leaving their hearts behind in the Ottumwa Cemetery with the remains of four of their children.

Michael W. Lemberger

Days Gone By

FROM ONE SIDE TO THE OTHER

In August, 1845, David Armstrong, the first surveyor in what was just a little hamlet with a few log cabins, surveyed the rapids named in honor of Chief Appanoose. It is hard to visualize what the Des Moines River was like those many years ago, as a river is a living thing and constantly changing course unless its energy is harnessed.

We do know a large island — Appanoose Island, also named for Chief Appanoose, who had resided there with his band, located where Fareway and the South Ottumwa Bank are now located — divided the river. The north channel contained the rapids, which forced steamboats to take the south channel. (The south channel was filled in even before the Ottumwa Coal Palace was a gleam in Peter Ballingall's eye.)

The findings of the survey of the Appanoose Rapids "ascertained that there passed the rapids every minute 42,000 cubic feet of water, a sufficient quantity to fill a lock 42 feet wide." It also was determined that there was a fall of four feet in a mile, enabling a five-foot high dam to allow a rise and fall of 6 feet 10 inches. As the years passed, the river changed course while quantities of rock were quarried from it, leaving the rapids as nothing but a piece of history to be ruminated on.

An enterprising carpenter named John C. Prosser, born in South Wales in 1820, traveled from Pennsylvania and arrived in Ottumwa June 13, 1856. In the Pickwick area of the south side, he purchased the Market Street ferry along with property which became Riverside Park. He operated the ferry for ten years before opening a mill at Port Richmond, a tiny settlement about one mile southwest of Pickwick, and another on Soap Creek.

It was John Overman, arriving from Indiana in 1845, who operated the ferry at the Port Richmond settlement located where Richmond and Ferry Streets intersect in Ottumwa. Why the name "Richmond" was chosen has been lost to time, but as the settlers named areas after birthplaces, and many of these families originated in Virginia, it is more than likely it is the namesake of that town in Virginia.

This ferry traveled between the little port and Central Addition, with another ferry operating between Central Addition and the foot of Wapello Street on the north side. Mr. Overman operated this ferry for eight years while continuing to farm. He was active in south side affairs, serving as a school board vice president, road supervisor and constable. John C. Prosser's son, also John C., later operated this ferry for two years while he farmed. John Overman is remembered today through his namesake, Overman Avenue.

Operating these ferries across the south channel left the operators open for much excitement dealing with the rapids as well as disgruntled riverboat captains when their boats became entangled with the chains and ropes of the ferries. The captains had axe men at the ready to cut the ferries loose from the boats. In October, 1861, it was John Prosser's Market Street ferry, breaking an oar while crossing the river, which was carried down the rapids as far as the "pork houses" before it could be stopped, leaving a passenger overboard who fell during the rapid descent. This passenger was one of the lucky ones rescued, as lives were lost on these rapids.

It cannot be forgotten that operating these ferries was a profit-making enterprise with tolls to be paid. It cost the south side farmers either "eight dozen eggs" or "pounds of butter" to cross the river to get their goods to market.

And many Ottumwans on the north side of the river were awakened from sleep as the southerly breezes carried the wail, "Over," yelled by travelers for a ferry to take them across.

Lemberger collection

Original dam across the Des Moines River at Ottumwa, under construction

Days Gone By

"WENT RAVEN MAD"

It didn't take the early settlers long to learn that the clear, beautiful and tranquil Des Moines River had a split personality and was prone to great flooding, as the swift current made her way southeast to the Mississippi. With heavy spring rains and without notice, she could quickly change into a raging demon, usurping homes and fields while gorging on the settlers' hard work in her frenzy racing south. Such were the great floods of 1851 which ripped through the state three times beginning in early June.

In a letter written July 13, 1851 from Wapello County by Lorenzo Warner to his brother in Ohio, he penned the following, in part: "We got your letter out of the office the 9th day of July. We was so glad to hear from you. We was afraid that you was all drowned in the mighty floods. My papers state that 4 persons was drowned in the Des Moines River and also Mr. Davis was drowned in Bluf Crick last Saturday. He was not found until.....three days afterward. He was to have been married on Sunday. D. was a natural swimmer. It was supposed that his horse went into a hole that was washed out and ... over his head and struck him on his head with his foot. Mr. D's skull was cracked. Now I will tell you how the farming business is going on. Well, it has rained ever since you left here. The Des Moines River has went raven mad. She has drove all the farmers out of the bottoms. The inhabitants of Eddyville has had to retreat three times this summer to the sandy hills. The waters has been so high that the fish could eat off the counters in the storehouses, the backhouses and the chicken houses. I expect that all the bridges is gone in the state. The water rose five or six feet higher than the gray bridge. All the mills was stopped grinding from the big waters so that the inhabitants was out of (flour)… Such a grinding on hand mills, coffee mills and pounding out hominy. .... Farming is bad. The boys quit planting the eighth of July. They have planted the field two or three times. It has rained so hard it has washed up the corn and drowned it. The prospects of corn is awful. All of the bottom farms are destroyed, which is about one third of the farms in the Ioway."

The 1851 flood was recalled in 1914 by Frank McMillan. He told of the families living near Cliffland, who, like those in Eddyville, had to abandon their property three times. They escaped by crossing the raging river to the other side, because the bluffs behind their farms were too wooded to climb. In doing this, nineteen head of sheep were lost. Hogs and cattle were tied to the back of boats and barges as they swam across, with the cattle losing all of the skin from their legs due to the swift current.

It was not until the beginning of August that all was normal again – with the farmers once more feeling safe as they viewed the clear, singing river, as the swift current continued its ageless course southeasterly.

Lemberger collection

This view of south Ottumwa from the north side of the Des Moines River was taken during the 1903 flood. No photographs are known to exist of the flood of 1851.

Days Gone By

GREAT AMERICAN HOG DRIVES

The western movies give us a good idea of what it was like to drive herds of cattle to the rail-head or to market, but there has never been a movie made of great herds of hogs being driven to market. Maybe because it would not conjure up many romantic images within our imaginations of a "hog boy" softly strumming a guitar under a starlit sky, soothing an oinking herd.

Though supplemented by local game and in-season fruits and vegetables, "hog and hominy" was the prevalent diet for our pioneer farmer ancestors. With little thought given to their life styles and their approach to animal husbandry, we do not realize that in the beginning there were no packing houses, and the farmers were left with the dilemma of what to do with the hogs they raised to sell. Entrepreneurs were at the ready, as in the case of N. D. Earl, who kept a general store in Dahlonega. Earl bought hogs from farmers near and far before a packing house was established in Dahlonega or Ottumwa. At this time Dahlonega was larger than Ottumwa.

So what did N. D. Earl do with the hogs in the days before packing plants? He drove them to Keokuk, of course, taking from ten days to two weeks to make the trip. That must have been a sight, and one wonders how many hands it took to drive them, as it is reported that there were times when he had a herd of as many as one thousand, so they were not loaded up in wagons and hauled away. The sights and sounds of this are hard to imagine. As farmers know, the hog is the brightest of farm animals, as well as the most stubborn, unless compared with a horse that doesn't want to be saddled. The hog's beady eyes can read minds, and that is when its independence takes over, dodging and darting while squealing all of the time. The polar bear is considered the most dangerous animal on earth, but farmers know this is not true: The most dangerous animal is the farrowing sow.

Mr. Earl not only owned the general store and dealt in hogs, but also was a local banker for those who wished him to hold their money from the sale of their hogs, drawing money from him as needed. Farmers charged merchandise from his store, and accounts were settled once a year.

It was much easier to drive sheep to market. A leader is coaxed to proceed and upon stepping forward, the rest of the sheep follow. This photograph shows sheep being "led to the slaughter" down the middle of a tree-shrouded East Second Street

A herd of sheep is driven down East Second Street on the way to the John Morrell & Co. packing house, in 1885.

on their way to John Morrell & Co., with the only human in sight an isolated figure on the sidewalk. Mr. Ham is too smart to be a part of this much quieter scene, and no comparable photograph is known to exist of hogs being driven to market.

Shortly after Mr. Earl was in business herding hogs, there was a Shepherd, named John R. who had a "ranch" at the corner of Washington and Main Streets, which he named Shepherd's Ranch, dealing in everything a successful farmer would need, as well as offering grain and use of a stable. When this Shepherd died in 1900, after having his "ranch" for forty years, one of his coffin bearers was R. Y. Cowherd!

PICK THE MONIKER

It is interesting to speculate how Ottumwa came to be named, and there are a number of theories as to "when, how, and what." But historians agree that the source closest to the time in question is generally the nearest to fact.

The April 21, 1887 edition of the Burlington *Post* ran an item which was picked up by *The Courier*, which in turn printed it on the following May 4.

The *Post* reported that a gentleman from Chariton, Missouri, had been told by a wise sage in the area that the commissioners, who would have been the Appanoose Rapids Company, and who had laid out the town of Ottumwa, agreed that the name

Lemberger collection

should be an Indian name and the name of a Chippewa chief, Ottomawonk, was considered, but some believing it too long, did not agree. When those in favor of "Ottomawonk" would not defer to those who wanted to shorten it to "Ottumwa", a commissioner in favor of the name "Ottumwa" grabbed a jug of whiskey and while walking away stated, "All of those in favor of calling the town 'Ottumwa' follow the jug" -- which a majority did.

In response to this version, *The Courier* received a letter from a gentleman by the name of W.B. Littleton, who wrote that he had met a man in Minneapolis, Minnesota by the last name of Janney, who had named the town. Mr. Janney told him that sitting on a nail keg whittling the pith from his corn cob pipe while consuming "fire water," as a meeting was in session in a log cabin on Main Street to name the town, the Indian name "Ottum.wa.nock" was mentioned. Mr. Janney, seeing a way to fame, stood up and suggested the "nock" be left off and the town named "Ottumwa." All were in favor and Mr. Janney's moniker was accepted.

What the two above accounts have in common is the fact that the "hair of the dog" is in evidence, which, no doubt, is responsible for those being nothing but "tales."

It is left to one of Ottumwa's first settlers, Dr. C.C. Warden, who arrived here July 2, 1843 and is considered by historians as a credible and primary source, to tell the *Courier* the truth of the matter: He relates that the "main trail from the Indian settlements on the Skunk River and Keokuk's camp on the prairie south of the river near the old town of Iowaville, crossed the Des Moines River at this place, and was known to the Indians as "Ot-tum-wi-e-nock," meaning rapid or swift water and hence "bad" crossing. This being so, it was natural and appropriate that the town company should name the town after it, and they did so."

Dr. Warden goes on to tell that the name was changed to Louisville, but changed back again to "Ottumwa." To those who had heard it spoken "in the soft, guttural tones" of the Indians, Dr. Warden believes that a mistake was made in shortening it from the original.

Dr. Warden's version, with its meaning, has stood the test of time without the "hair of the dog."

Days Gone By

CABIN AMONG THE TREES:
A Cool and Quiet Place

Among the trees in Ottumwa's Memorial Park is a cabin which appears as if the park had been built around it. But this little cabin could tell tales of travel before it nestled down in the park.

It was actually erected in the early years of the 1850s in the fledgling community of Mt. Pleasant by an adventurer who had already traveled by ox and mule team from Plymouth, New Hampshire to San Francisco with his father, where they built the first toll bridge across the Sacramento River. They then returned to Boston by ship before coming west.

Joseph Henry Merrill started his life of adventure going from one coast to the other at the age of twenty-one. Though he spent most of his business career in the wholesale grocery business, he was working for the Chicago, Burlington and Quincy Railroad in Mt. Pleasant in 1858. He and his wife, whom he had married in 1854 before coming west again in 1855, welcomed into the cabin they had built the second of their five children, a son, Herman W. Merrill, on January 15, 1858.

1858 was a record year for Iowa migration as well as for Des Moines River steam boating. It was also the year J. H. Merrill, with a partner, Charles W. Kittridge, loaded the steamboat *Clara Hines* in St. Louis with salt they had purchased for 90 cents a sack. Upon the arrival at the dock in Ottumwa at the foot of Court and Front (Main) Streets, they intended to sell the salt for $2.25 a sack, once their business of Merrill & Kittridge was opened a few days later.

The trip from St. Louis was fraught with impediments of many kinds for steamboats and the two young entrepreneurs, with their cargo, counted on an experienced captain to surmount the obstacles of sandbars and snags. In addition, they faced the obstacle of dams across the Des Moines, placed there by millers. The dams challenged the skills of every steamboat captain, charging the dams with "flying" over them or breaking through. If this was accomplished without too much damage, one hoped that another boat of this genre was not coming from the opposite direction, as it was nearly impossible for the two to pass successfully. Not depending on the costly, unreliability of steamboat shipping on the Des Moines River after this adventure, Merrill and Kittridge, acting as their own teamsters, brought their goods from Keokuk and Burlington by wagon until Ottumwa became the terminus of the railroad from Burlington in 1859.

Kittridge left for the Civil War in 1861, leaving Merrill alone to operate the business until Samuel Mahon became a partner after the war. The partnership was dissolved in 1901, when Joseph was secure in his son's knowledge of the business and embarked on a partnership with Herman, as J. H. Merrill & Co., which became the largest wholesale grocery business in this part of the state.

J. H. Merrill passed away in 1911 leaving the business in the very capable hands of his son. It was his son, Herman, who removed the cabin home of his birth to a bucolic setting behind his own home at 401 North Green, surrounding it with meandering paths of wild flowers, hollyhocks, delphiniums and other shrubs and plantings, where it became a source of quiet rest and cool comfort for summer family gatherings, as he filled it with relics from their pioneer past.

Mr. Merrill later presented the cabin to the city park system for all to enjoy. It resides on the Elm Street side of Memorial Park as a symbol of our own ancestors' new life on the Iowa Prairie. It is available for use year round by contacting the city parks department for reservations.

Lemberger collection

Merrill Log cabin behind the Merrill home on North Green Street, before it was moved to Memorial Park

Days Gone By

Michael W. Lemberger

A BED AND BREAKFAST

A very old, obscure, one-story home on a large lot in south Ottumwa holds a secret and a unique history. The house at 505 Burrhus Street has changed over the decades, hiding its age. A concrete basement floor, poured in the early 1940s, covers the original dirt floor. New floors have also been laid over the original plank flooring on the main level, hiding the secret – which can now only be seen from the underside and viewed from the basement. For in the original planking are not one, but two trap doors which opened to the basement. They were so craftly built in the plank flooring that they were unidentifiable when viewed from the top, before the new flooring was laid. Also in the basement is a most intriguing, sophisticated, walled-up brick entrance to what appears to have been a tunnel.

This historic house was part of a farm owned originally by Jane Overman, who died in 1857. Legend states her son John, who owned and operated the ferry between Port Richmond (South Ottumwa) and the north side of the Des Moines River, had a false bottom built in the ferry boat to transport runaway slaves from one side of the river to the other. The Overmans were members of the Society of Friends, commonly known as Quakers. This is very strong evidence that the legend was based on truth, as the Quakers and the Congregationalists were the most active organized groups helping slaves to freedom. This, in connection with the surreptitious trap doors in the Overman home, as well as an apparent tunnel opening leading toward the river, is overwhelming circumstantial evidence that the modest home at 505 Burrhus Street was indeed a part of the underground railroad. The channel of the Des Moines River has changed dramatically, but in those days, the tunnel did not have to go far before coming to the river.

Sue Parrish

There would have been help on the north side of the river. One of Ottumwa's founders, Reverend Benjamin Spaulding, who organized the First Congregational Church in Ottumwa in 1846, was a member of what was called the Iowa Band. The Iowa Band was a group of Congregational ministers who came to Iowa to collectively found a college, now Grinnell College, and each organize a church. There can be no doubt that Spaulding and his father-in-law, another Ottumwa founder and Congregationalist, and Ottumwa's first shoemaker, Samuel S. Norris, were active in this endeavor. Norris "was an uncompromising Abolitionist, and his house was one of the stations on the Underground Railroad." (Coincidently, Spaulding's sister married Norris's son.) The Spaulding residence and the Samuel Norris residence were across College Street from each other, facing East Second Street.

We will never know the number of people involved in transporting escaped slaves to safety in the North, because of the secrecy involved. In an April, 1934 issue of *The Courier*, an article by Eudora Nosler was quoted: "About the year 1859, as I recall it, there were mysterious happenings at my father's house. One dark night a man by the name of Chapman coming from Wayne County, on the Missouri line, made his appearance at the door— apparently not expected. My father was called to the barn, the man went away and the next day food was carried to the barn. We children were forbidden to go near the place, but curiosity got the better of my brother and myself, and peering through a crevice, we saw sitting on the hay, a colored person — a black man." She goes on to relate that later she overheard her father telling her mother he had crossed the Skunk River and met a man by the name of Johnson at Moffit's mill, and he "guessed Johnson would get him through."

With the Quaker settlements in Oskaloosa and New Sharon, and the founder of Grinnell, Josiah B. Grinnell, a Congregationalist and known abolitionist, Ottumwa's Quakers and Congregationalists were in an ideal position to provide a station stop for this unique railroad, as runaways made their way north through Iowa from New Salem to Grinnell and other points north. Though the evidence is only circumstantial, it seems likely that the little house nestled among the trees on Burrhus Street provided a bed and breakfast for very scared and weary travelers.

Harvey Grooms shows the underside of the trap door at 505 Burrhus.

Michael W. Lemberger

CALL TO ARMS

As a new day dawned on the morning of April 12, 1861, Spring was in full glory in Wapello County with the greening of the wildflower-covered prairies. As everyone began their chores on this new day, little did the prairie towns of Iowa know that hundreds of miles away the day had come which many feared. The American Civil War began with the firing on Fort Sumter, South Carolina by southern rebels during the early morning hours of April 12. The fort surrendered the following day. The war would try their hearts and souls and culminate almost four years to the day later with a first in American history: the assassination of an American president.

Iowa organizations quickly offered their services to the governor with Guardsmen gathering in Keokuk. The 1st Iowa Volunteer Infantry of Iowa Guardsmen was organized, with Wapello County volunteers being attached to ten companies from towns outside of the county. The regiment was mustered in for three months of active duty May 14, 1861. The government issued them U.S. model 1829 flintlock rifles and no uniforms, which later gave them the distinction of being called "the ragamuffin unit of the army." Before the regiment was transferred to Hannibal, Missouri in June, their time was spent not only drilling and electing officers, but taking part in a great many fights with southern sympathizers in and around Keokuk.

At that time, most believed it wouldn't take long to quell the rebellion and return to the comforts of home, as expressed by one nineteen year old.: "I expect I will be in the war. Nobody thinks it will last long; some say it won't last over ninety days." This was in response to dire predictions from his grandfather, "…I have been expecting war for twenty years. This country has all gone to smash; the constitution is of no use any more… the government Washington gave us is busted to pieces. There never will be any more such good times as there use to be; about everybody's going to get killed unless something stops it…"

The 1st Iowa was attached to the command of Brigadier General Nathaniel Lyon, who was quickly chasing the Missouri State Guard into the southwestern part of Missouri, trying to retain control of this border state. With the advance, the Iowans had resorted to sending home for more clothing or buying clothing themselves. The men were molested during rest periods by wood ticks, seed ticks, lice and the bed bugs living in the soil of the area. As if that wasn't enough, there were chiggers, fleas, flies and mosquitoes to contend with. To top it all off, they had no stockings and had resorted to filling their shoes with soap. With this there was good to come: After the long march, the soap had healed them of any corns!

This march through Missouri culminated in the Battle of Wilson's Creek on August 10, 1861, south of Springfield, Missouri, in which General Lyon was killed. Both sides claimed victory, leaving the Union forces retreating unmolested. All Confederate supplies were destroyed, with losses of approximately 2,500 on each side. The Union gained their objective of opening up a road to Springfield, Missouri which had been blocked by the rebels, but the rebels were now in control of southern Missouri.

As they marched toward Wilson's Creek, the 1st Iowa soon learned the war was not going to be over in ninety days, and they were deeply shocked at the Union loss at the Battle of Bull Run in July. Shortly after this battle, they were mustered out and those from Wapello County quickly reenlisted in other companies to go on to make names for themselves in the great Western Campaign.

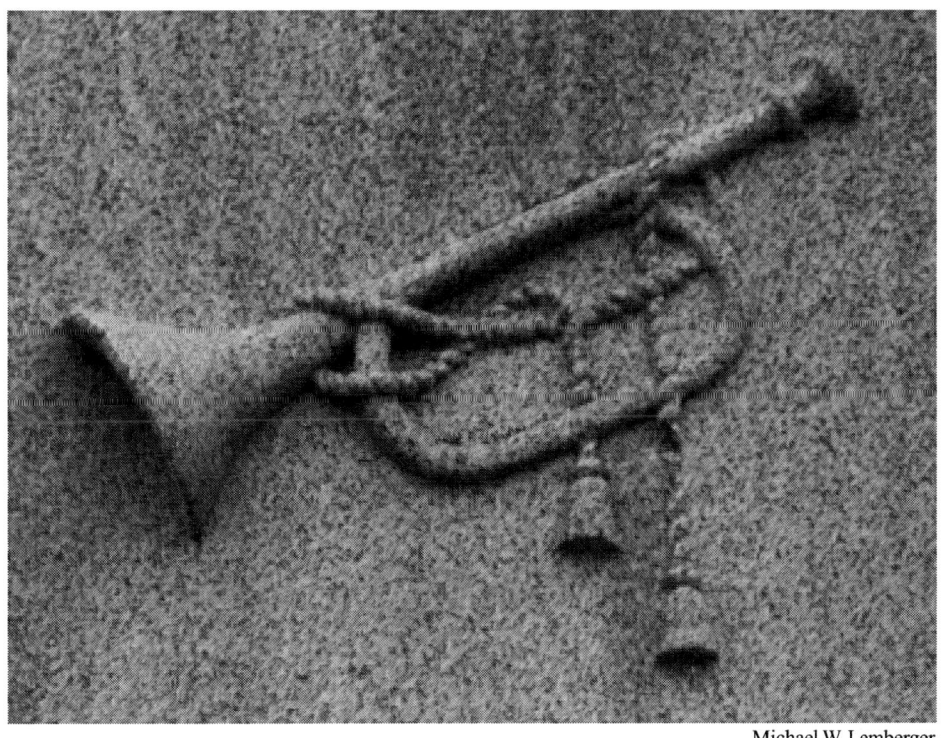

Michael W. Lemberger

Days Gone By

ON THE TENNESSEE RIVER

April 6, 1862 gave the promise of being a beautiful Sunday on the west bank of the Tennessee River in southwest Tennessee. It was five days before the first anniversary of the firing on Ft. Sumter. As the first blush of sunrise appeared, its rays shone on a small Methodist church named Shiloh, after an ancient center of worship in Israel. It was part of an enclave around a steamboat landing called Pittsburg Landing, which also included a small pond and a peach orchard in bloom. However, along with the rising sun at 6:00 a.m. came the rebel yell under the leadership of Gen. Sydney Johnston — a yell used all through the war and orchestrated to terrorize the enemy — and the Battle of Shiloh began. Covering two days, it would become the bloodiest battle in the Civil War to that time, with the total of killed and injured at 23,716.

The 7th and 8th Iowa Infantries, with their many Wapello County residents, will always be remembered for trying to hold the stretch of ground Grant stated must be held "at all cost." And hold they tried. It became known as "The Hornet's Nest" for the incessant firing that sounded like thousands of hornets -- hornets that would be responsible for the deaths of so many. This command, under Benjamin Prentiss, held during twelve assaults, with Prentiss finally surrendering after Grant had been given enough time to form a line of siege guns guarding Pittsburg Landing for reinforcements.

Company "F" of the 7th Iowa was comprised of Wapello County boys who had been in the service for eight months and had seen two other battles. They were left with a total dead of 300 out of 884 men by the end of this battle, a battle in which they showed exceptional courage.

Godfrey Lewis of Dahlonega was one of the lucky ones. He, like many others, had come down with a fever and had been discharged on April 2. Amos Reed of Ottumwa, wounded, died of his wounds May 11, while Samuel Ream and Joseph Sidney survived theirs. Officers from Ottumwa, Charles Kitteredge and Samuel Mahon, survived the battle, as did Thomas Barnes of Kirkville.

Iowa lost more lives in the battle of Shiloh than any other state involved. The 8th Iowa took the brunt of the fight over this ground and fought into the night until they were surrounded. Those left alive were taken prisoner.

Grant himself was wounded on the afternoon of the first day and was carried to a boat at Pittsburg Landing, leading to the erroneous tale perpetuated by his detractors

— one of many — that he had been carried off the field drunk.

This battle for control of the Mississippi Valley brought the unbeatable team of Ulysses S. Grant and William T. Sherman together for the first time; their later tactics forever altered the fighting of wars. The Battle of Shiloh was also the first time in history that a field hospital tent was set up on the field of battle, and it was the only battle during the entire rebellion in which a Confederate commanding officer was killed, when Gen. Johnston bled to death April 6 while his personal physician was tending other wounded.

This fight, won by the Union, was the first step in dividing the south in half by controlling the Mississippi and its valley. The Iowans followed Grant south, and the fight for the Mississippi culminated with the fall of Vicksburg the next year. On July 4, General John Pemberton surrendered the city to Grant, after Sherman had prophesied, "This is a death struggle, and will be terrible." Grant requested an unconditional surrender, but relented and paroled Pemberton's troops.

The Battle of Shiloh, or Pittsburg Landing, will always be remembered for the evening of April 7, 1862 with its peach orchard devoid of all blossoms and its pond running red with blood from the north and the south, as both sides sought relief from their wounds.

Michael W. Lemberger

Days Gone By

TALES FROM VICKSBURG

Seneca Brown Thrall, son of the renowned scientist and medical doctor H.L. Thrall of Kenyon College, Ohio, was born in Utica, Ohio in 1832 and graduated in 1853 from the University of New York -- following in his father's footsteps. He married Mary Brooks of Columbus, Ohio, whom he fondly called "Mollie," and as newlyweds, the couple arrived in Ottumwa in 1856 to set up his medical practice and become part of the burgeoning Ottumwa social set.

With the outbreak of the Civil War, it was not long before Dr. Thrall's services were needed. In February, 1862, he became a surgeon at the military hospital in Keokuk. In November of that year he was commissioned Assistant Surgeon to the 13th Iowa Volunteers, serving with them until May, 1864. During his time in service he wrote nearly daily to Mollie, leaving us with a very vivid and colorful account of his life in the 17th Corps, 13th Iowa.

The following excerpt was written from Vicksburg, Mississippi and dated August 2, 1863. Gen. U.S. Grant had taken control of Vicksburg on July 4, after a tough forty-seven day siege.

"…We are camped about a mile and a half north, or up the river, from the courthouse. The whole country is hill and ravine, hill and ravine. The roughest place I ever saw in which to build a town. Worse, far worse than Keokuk, Burlington or Muscatine. <u>Worse</u> than the hills and ravines back of our house, McElroys, Lawrence and Merrills. The roof of a two story house on one lot is frequently many feet below the foundation of a house only 20 feet away on the adjoining lot. There are a few fine mansions yet, as we would naturally expect. The town presents the appearance of dilapidation and neglect. It appears that it had been rented several years and the repairs entirely neglected. A large majority of the houses show marks of entrance of one or more balls, yet externally do not show much damage, although the inside arrangements (plastering, partitions and floors) seriously injured. I have only <u>seen</u> <u>two</u> houses which seem to have been literally knocked to pieces by our shells or balls. Yesterday I counted on one side of the depot 18 shot holes, yet it was not much injured."

During the siege, the residents of Vicksburg had set up homes in caves, life in which is very graphically depicted by Mary Chestnut, wife of Confederate General James Chestnut, Jr., in the book *A Diary from Dixie*. Dr. Thrall continues his letter with a description of these caves:

"The sides of the hills are full of caves, as you have read in papers; some of them quite nicely furnished and quite pleasant… A number of these caves <u>ought</u> to be preserved, as most interesting mementoes, and I hope it will be done. They afforded perfect safety to thousands and had I lived here and built one, I should keep it to show to future generations as a visible evidence of what their <u>celebrated ancestors</u> had done…"

After he was mustered out, Dr. Thrall returned to his Ottumwa medical practice. He and Mollie raised three children, and Mollie — Mary Brooks Thrall — was instrumental in the building of the Ottumwa Hospital on East Second Street.

Michael W. Lemberger

APRIL MEMORIES

Wapello County's Civil War veterans always remembered the month of April – especially those of the 7th Iowa who became part of the 36th Iowa after Shiloh. The first shots of the war were fired during the month of April; the Battle of Shiloh occurred during April; Lee surrendered in April and President Abraham Lincoln was mortally wounded on Good Friday, April 14. But most importantly to those of the 36th Iowa — the soldiers who survived the battle of Mark's Mill were taken prisoner during the month of April.

Ottumwan Burn Bannister wrote in his synopsis of the events of April 25, 1864, "If I were asked to suggest a tragic day in the history of Wapello County, I would choose the date of Monday, April 25, 1864…."

April 25, 1864 began as a cold and damp spring morning near the edge of a pine woods in Bradley County, Arkansas. It would be the last morning a majority of the 36th Iowa would ever see. By 9:30 a.m., 8,000 Confederates had descended on the unsuspecting train of 240 empty wagons going for supplies. By the middle of the afternoon, all of the 36th Iowa, along with the 43rd Indiana, were either dead or taken prisoner as a result of what became known as the Battle of Mark's Mill.

They fought until their ammunition was exhausted, and then they fought in hand-to-hand combat, giving up only when overcome by the sheer weight of the number of the enemy. A total of 18 officers and 371 enlisted men of the 36th were captured and moved to Camp Ford in Tyler, Texas, including brothers Jacob and John Breon of Keokuk County and Major A.H. Hamilton of Ottumwa. At Camp Ford, 54 died in captivity, including the Breon brothers.

Those who were severely wounded were immediately paroled, including Lt. Col. F.M. Drake of Centerville, who became Governor of Iowa and has been honored by a university and a community bearing his name: Drake University and Drakesville, Iowa.

Major Hamilton escaped on July 23 with Captains John Lambert and Allen Miller. They made their way to Little Rock, Arkansas, where the two captains succumbed to the hardship of their escape. Major Hamilton recuperated from his ordeal and rejoined the service.

Camp Ford, near Tyler, Texas, was originally a training camp for Confederate soldiers, but it was converted to a prisoner of war camp for Union soldiers during the

Sue Parrish

**Graves of Union and Confederate soldiers at
Rock Island Arsenal National Cemetery**

Michael W. Lemberger

summer of 1863. By the time the 36th Iowa had arrived on noon Sunday, May 15, 1864, a routine had been established by other prisoners, who had constructed their own shelter of burrows, brush arbors, blanket tents or log huts. As there was a spring in a corner of the camp, there was a constant supply of water in this six-plus acre prison, making for more favorable conditions than in other prisoner of war camps. Still, conditions for the prisoners were deplorable at best. Prisoner of war exchanges alleviated crowded conditions to a certain extent, but according to Josiah Young of Albia, it was a "dreadful place."

Young described rations as "about one-quarter of a pound of beef per man per day. That is when the authorities are in good humor, and they were nearly always mad. They punished the whole camp when Yanks escaped by withholding our rations. The ration of corn meal was a pint per day." This account was followed later with, "The rations issued by the authorities were not sufficient to gratify the natural appetite of well men and many died."

Many soldiers augmented their diet by making trinkets and selling them for groceries brought by civilians in the surrounding area and made available at Camp Ford. Members of the 36th Iowa carved chess pieces to barter and sell.

On February 27, 1865, the prisoners were exchanged in New Orleans and drew their pay. The bodies of those who died at Camp Ford were later removed to Alexandria National Cemetery in Pineville, Louisiana.

"KISS MY SWEET LITTLE BOYS FOR ME"

The 8th Iowa Cavalry was organized in Davenport in September 1863 and assigned to the Army of the Cumberland. The 8th left on October 17, arriving in Louisville on October 21, 1863 and in Nashville November 17. They saw little action during the winter of 1863-1864 and remained on guard and garrison duty. But this was to change. They were in the front of Sherman's Atlanta Campaign and were fearless. They are best known for their raid to cut the Atlanta and Macon Railroad near Lovejoy's Station, Georgia.

One of the valiant soldiers of the 8th Iowa was Sgt. Christopher Ross Kinkade of Eddyville, born in Kentucky in 1832. He was a plasterer by profession; he married Armida "Mid" Catherine Nosler, the daughter of a local doctor, and was raising a family. He was under the command of Col. Joseph B. Dorr, who had distinguished himself at the Battle of Shiloh. "Mid" saved nearly all of his letters to her, which gives us a taste of the soldier's life with the 8th Iowa Cavalry. He ended nearly all of his letters with, "Kiss my sweet little boys for me."

The following letter dated June 20, 1864, is one of the last letters remaining in the collection.

"My dear wife and children: I have not received a letter from you since I wrote, but I am looking for one every day. I am well and hope this may find you well. Mid, I have got to think I can stand anything. It has rained on us for 5 days and nights without intermission. This is true, we have been having some awful hard fighting this past week. Sherman drove the Rebs seven miles yesterday. He has been pushing them harder than he would have done because the river was up so they couldn't cross, but they got some pontoons laid yesterday and I tell you they used them too well.

"Cap and McDobe and all from Eddyville that are with us are well. There is only 20 men left in our company. I am the only Sgt. With the camp. McDobe and Dean the only Corpl. Sgt. Craig is sent back to Kingston sick. He is not very bad. (Lt. Ware started to Kingston this morning sick.) He has been off duty for over a week laying around Cap got tired of it and ordered him to the rear. (About Craig not Ware.) He is the most perfect boor I ever seen to pretend to be a man at all.

"I wrote you in the last letter that our brigade had been ordered to the rear. So we had, but the Reb cavalry appeared in force on our right center and we were ordered out to drive them back and here we are yet. I have not the least idea when we will be sent back now. Company B & L & D was on picket three days and nights, just came in camp yesterday, but we live very well now. Huckleberry and dew berries are very plenty and ripe. We have lots of sugar and of course a pot of stewed fruit sweetened or thickened with sugar with our usual allowance of hard tack and sow belly- - Tell Ebb and George if they cannot write they might roll up a paper once in a while and send to Hen or I, we would be glad to get them. Paper cannot be had on these mountains. I must close, the camp is ordered out to graze our horses. We can see across the river to Atlanta from the top of Lost Mountain. Kiss the boys for me, write soon. Give my respects to enquiring friends. In haste yours as ever, most affectionately.

"C.R. Kinkade P.S. Tell Maggie Barker I see her brother every day nearly. I have not got acquainted with him yet, but I know him when I see him. CRK"

Christopher Ross Kinkade was killed October 30, 1864 during an encounter with Confederate General John Bell Hood's forces along the Tennessee River near Florence, Alabama.

Days Gone By

BRAVERY KNOWS NO COLOR

Two men buried in Ottumwa — one black and one white — received the Congressional Medal of Honor for their bravery during the Civil War: James Daniel Gardner, black, and Leonidas M. Godley, white.

General Grant had full confidence in what were then refered to as colored troops, and he believed they were a great asset to the Union. "By arming the Negro we have added a powerful ally. They will make good soldiers and taking them from the enemy weakens him in the same proportion they strengthen us."

Not all of the top command agreed, but Major General Benjamin Butler specifically chose the black 36th U.S. Colored Infantry, because he believed they could do the task placed before him. One of these black infantrymen, James Daniel Gardner, born in Virginia in 1839, had joined the 2nd North Carolina Colored Infantry in 1863 and helped to prove General Butler correct in his assessment.

Under the command of General Butler against the forces of Generals Lee and Ewell, the Union won a very hard-fought battle known as New Market Heights or Chaffin's Farm on September 29, 1864. This was part of the Richmond-Petersburg Campaign begun in June, 1864 with one of the bloodiest battles in American history, Cold Harbor, which brought Grant to tears.

During the Battle of New Market Heights, James Gardner rushed in advance of his brigade to rally the troops, after the blacks had received terrible losses. Rallied, the troops took the ground as Gardner ran his bayonet through a rebel officer. The accomplishment of these black troops and General Butler's confidence in them is remembered to this day.

Gardner, one of 23 blacks to receive the Medal of Honor during that war, out of 173,000 black soldiers in the Union Army, settled in Ottumwa. He married and became a Catholic missionary. While on a missionary trip he died in Pennsylvania, ironically on the forty-first anniversary of the Battle of New Market Heights. He is buried in Calvary Cemetery.

Leonidas M. Godley of Ashland, a long forgotten community south of Agency, was wounded severely during the siege of Vicksburg May 22, 1863. A member of the 22nd Iowa, he didn't hear the command to halt, and overran one of the enemy's works far ahead of his regiment, receiving three very serious injuries: two to his left leg and one to his right breast with the musket ball passing through and exiting out the shoulder blade. After lying in the hot Mississippi sun all day, he was taken prisoner. His injuries were so severe that his left leg was amputated without the luxury of anesthesia, a common event during the war. Despite this, however, he said he was well treated by the Confederates. After the amputation in the field, he was taken by lumber wagon to a residence serving as a hospital, which was immediately shelled by the Union forces, causing the Confederates to leave. Finally discovered by these forces, he was sent to St. Louis and discharged on September 4, 1863.

After his return home to Ashland, three more inches of his leg were amputated. Since he was no longer able to pursue his carpentry profession, he turned to politics and business. He moved to Ottumwa in 1874 and was elected to the office of County Clerk, a position he held for seven consecutive terms. He was then appointed a revenue agent in 1883, and the following year, a deputy in the same office.

He received the Medal of Honor for leading the assault on the parapet and receiving the three wounds during the commission of taking it. He died May 23, 1904 and is buried in Ottumwa Cemetery.

ANECDOTES AND PETTICOATS

On March 17, 1884 a charter was issued for the Cloutman Post of the Grand Army of the Republic in memory of Capt. Charles C. Cloutman, the first Ottumwan to fall in battle during the Civil War. Mr. Cloutman raised his own company, Co. K, 2nd Iowa, and was commissioned as a Captain by Governor Kirkwood. Mr. Cloutman lost his life while leading his company in a charge during the fall of Fort Donelson, Tennessee.

Like many of Wapello County's volunteers, Charles Cloutman was born elsewhere, in Conway, New Hampshire. He married Rachel Scott, another Iowa transplant and cousin of General Winfield Scott, in Burlington in 1850. He was a blacksmith by trade. His death on February 15, 1862 left his wife, Rachel and four children, including his namesake, Charles, who was born after his death.

The first local president of the Cloutman Post, Grand Army of the Republic, Woman's Relief Corps was Lauretta Love Cowles. When the Civil War broke out, the girls' college she was attending in Quincy, Illinois closed its doors, and she returned to her parents' home in LaClede, Missouri, near Chillicothe. Her father, William R. Love, and his business partner, John F. Pershing, operated a general store and post office there. Mr. Pershing's son, John J., would later become chief of the American Expeditionary forces during World War I.

Lauretta's father became a recruiting officer for the Union's 18th Missouri, but later joined the 87th Missouri, known as the famous Blackhawk Cavalry. Being a border state, Missouri was a dangerous place for an abolitionist to live, as Lauretta learned by experience. On June 14, 1864, at four o'clock in the afternoon, a band of thirty guerrillas rode into LaClede under the command of Capt. Clifton Holtzclaw.

Lemberger collection

In 1930, six members of Cloutman Post #69, with a combined age of 574 years, posed for this photo. The members were identifed as Levi C. Traul, John C. Hueston, William H. Cline, J. L. Lemberger, J. W. Moore, and Reuben Ware.

Sue Parrish
Parrish collection

Lauretta Love Cowles

They were looking for two abolitionists: Lt. John Reynolds and Lauretta's father, Capt. W.R. Love, who was in LaClede recuperating from an illness. The raiders went to her father's store and began looting, during which two men were shot.

In the meantime, Capt. Love, accompanied by Lauretta, had been to the post office where he received $200 owed him. While crossing the square, he was ordered out of the square by the guerrillas. He was able to drop his purse containing the money in a log, hoping to retrieve it later. As Capt. Love was dressed in a white linen suit, he was not recognized, and when his daughter pleaded for him to be released for home using the excuse, "He is old and disabled," the guerrillas let him go with the promise from Lauretta that she would keep him home all night.

They retraced their steps, and as they neared the log, Lauretta loosened her skirt with its folds falling over the log, giving her the opportunity to pick up the money-filled purse within the skirt's folds, in clear view of the rebels. Earlier, two men had escaped, and they rode to Brookfield to warn the Union troops, who, in turn, hurried to LaClede by train, routing the guerrillas as the Loves were nearing their front gate.

Two abolitionists' lives were saved!

Miss Love married Daniel B. Cowles in 1868. Though he was from Minnesota, Cowles had been on patrol duty along the Tennessee River at Fort Donelson. His battalion — Brackett's — was moved to Minnesota where his company helped quell Indian uprisings and guarded emigrant trains west. He retired as a conductor for the CB&Q, and he was the commander of the Iowa department of the Grand Army of the Republic at the time of his death in 1925.

After the war, Lauretta's parents, Mr. and Mrs. Love, moved to Wapello County. They are buried in the Agency Cemetery, and Daniel and Lauretta Cowles rest in Ottumwa Cemetery.

There are many tales beneath the sod in Wapello County, never to be heard again.

DEAD MEN MEET

During the Civil War many personal encounters occurred which years later led to reunions of the blue and the gray. Such an event inspired the heartwarming article, *"Two Dead Men Meet"* in the October 27, 1892 issue of *The Ottumwa Evening Courier.*

James H. Coe of Ottumwa was born in New York and was not a resident of Wapello County until after the Civil War. As a native of New York, he enlisted in the 159th New York State Volunteers as a private. On September 19, 1864, he carried with him into the Battle of Winchester, Virginia — called the Third Battle of Winchester — a prayer book given him by his father, Rev. Jonathan Coe, with the following inscription: JAMES H. COE, From His Father, JONATHAN COE, Athens, NY., Jan. 25, 1864.

The Third Battle of Winchester, with General Sheridan's Union army outnumbering General Jubal Early's Confederates three to one, was the first battle in the Shenandoah Valley Campaign under the leadership of General Sheridan, which was to "lay waste" the bread basket of the Confederacy. "Nothing should be left to invite the enemy to return," Grant ordered. Sheridan told his men, "The people must be left with nothing but their eyes to weep." And that is all the Shenandoah Valley had left.

Coe was felled during the first charge, which rendered him unconscious with the appearance of death. As the Confederate line moved forward, John D. Pope of the 44th Georgia came across Coe's body, and as Pope's rifle was hot from firing, he bent down and picked up Coe's cold rifle. While stooping to pick up Coe's cartridges, he was shot through the shoulder with the ball coming out at the middle of his back. He fell over Coe's body,

Michael W. Lemberger

becoming unconscious himself and not rallying until the battle was over. As he awakened and struggled to his hands and knees, he noticed the prayer book, a New Testament, and a portfolio in Coe's haversack, which he pulled out and dragged along as he crawled away.

Years later, in 1872, Pope's conscience prevailed upon him to notify the parents of Coe to let them know how their son had died, as they both had been shot on the same spot. Using the information provided in the prayer book's inscription, he sent a letter to the Rev. and Mrs. Jonathan Coe. Fate intervened and John Pope never received the response from Mrs. Coe and her daughter, telling him that Jonathan Coe had died in 1866; to keep what he had found, if the items were beneficial to him; and that James Coe had survived.

Twenty years passed and James Coe was living in Ottumwa, rooming at 106 South Market and working as a foreman at the Chicago, Milwaukee & St. Paul roundhouse. He wondered if the rebel who had sent his mother the letter years ago was still living. He wrote a letter of inquiry to the return address on Pope's letter to Mrs. Coe, and to James Coe's delight, he received the following, in part:

"…..It would be one of the happiest hours of my life to grasp the hand of one whom I thought dead on the battle field. I earnestly request that you visit me at your earliest convenience and I will divide 'hardtack and sow belly' with you… You will find a hearty welcome from all ex-confederates… I prefer to see you face to face and extend to you the right hand of fellowship and good will…."

James Coe traveled to Douglasville, Georgia in October, 1892 to meet with John Pope. They fell into each other's arms, hugging and crying. Two men, who had officially never met, but whose blood had mingled together as they lay entwined, unconscious, on a battlefield, one in blue and the other in gray, appearing as dead men who had mortally wounded each other.

Michael W. Lemberger

GENERAL JAMES SHIELDS and MOLLY

General James Shields, the namesake for Ottumwa Council 888 of the Knights of Columbus, never lived in Ottumwa, but the city held close ties for him. Born in Ireland May 10, 1810, he set sail for America at the age of 16 and landed in New York in 1826. He was admitted to the New York Bar in 1832, but soon followed the migration west and found himself in Illinois. He was elected as a Jacksonian Democrat to the Illinois House of Representatives in 1836 and as State Auditor in 1839.

Also, at this time in Springfield was a gangly six-foot-four-inch lawyer who, being a Whig, wrote numerous satirical articles, along with other authors, under the pseudonym of Aunt Rebecca for the Whig newspaper *Sangamo Journal.* James Shields became the target of Aunt Rebecca's satire while Shields, as the state auditor, was remedying the state's abysmal finances. By stating that he demanded silver and gold for taxes instead of the devalued paper money, Shields deeply angered the Whigs, and the satire from the *Sangamo Journal* became especially derisive. Shields, demanding to know from the editor the author of these letters, was told the newspaper had no idea who had written them. Shields sent a scathing reply to Aunt Rebecca and both James Shields and Aunt Rebecca believed this was the end of it.

But "Aunt Rebecca" had a fiancée nicknamed Molly, who, with a friend, wrote a mocking poem to the newspaper explaining that Shields and Rebecca were to be married. That did it for Shields. Described as a "genial, but puffed-up man," he was beside himself with anger. Taking the blame for his fiancée, "Aunt Rebecca" (a.k.a. Abraham Lincoln) told the editor of the paper to inform Shields he had written the poem.

As a result, Lincoln found himself challenged by Shields to a duel. The person who is challenged has the choice of weapons, but Lincoln's first weapon of choice — an ax — was not allowed. Lincoln then chose cavalry broadswords

Lemberger collection
General James Shields

Sue Parrish

Mary Todd Lincoln

Lemberger collection

in the belief that he, being so tall with long arms, would have the advantage over Shields, who was a small man.

When the time came for the duel, with their sabers drawn out of their sheaths, Shields realized the advantage Lincoln had, but would not stop the duel. Lincoln returned his sword to its sheath and stated, " Mary Todd wrote those verses that infuriated you." Shields knew Mary Todd, as they were part of the same social circle, and Mary Todd actually liked Shields, describing him as "a kindhearted, impulsive Irishman, always creating a sensation and mirth by his drolleries." Those attending the duel broke out in laughter as Shields and Lincoln shook hands on the way to becoming close friends.

The winner of the duel would have been doomed in either case, as dueling was a hanging offense in Illinois – except that to avoid the authorities, the duel was actually held on an island in the Mississippi River.

James Shields had an illustrious career in public service and is the only man to have served in the United States Senate from three different states. His career included heroism in the Mexican War and the American Civil War, when his forces fought valiantly in June 1862 to expel "Stonewall" Jackson from the Shenandoah Valley. Though the Union forces routed Jackson at one point, they were unsuccessful this early in the war in taking over the valley.

Invited by Rev. John Kreckel in May 1879 to speak in Ottumwa on his "Reminiscences of the Mexican War," Shields gladly accepted. Not only was Kreckel a friend, but the visit would give him the opportunity to visit with his cousin Mary Tally, the benefactress of the Sisters of Humility, and his niece and adopted daughter, Mary Shields. After being in Ottumwa only five days, he suddenly became ill and died the evening of June 1, 1879.

General Shields said of Lincoln, " Lincoln was to the people of his nation what Beethoven was to music…If he had failed to become President, he would have been, no doubt, just as great; but only God would have appreciated him."

BITTERSWEET VICTORY

On the evening of April 14, 1865, an assassin's bullet struck its mark, and the assassin shouted in Latin "Death to Tyrants" as he fled Ford's Theater. The audience, including an Ottumwan, were stunned to realize they had been in attendance at the assassination of their victorious president, Abraham Lincoln, and could not save him. He had been shot as he sat in the presidential box with his wife, Mary. They were accompanied by Major Henry Rathbone and his fiancé, Clara Harris. Major Rathbone suffered a stab wound while trying to subdue the fleeing assassin.

Though the president clung to life until the next morning, fate's screws were

Lemberger collection

Abraham Lincoln, from an original negative taken by Matthew Brady

turning with an infection of evil set off by the twisted mind of the assassin, John Wilkes Booth, who sought revenge believing his act would bring him accolades of honor.

General John M. Hedrick of Ottumwa was in Washington D.C. on military business, a court-martial, when he attended Ford's Theater that evening. Hedrick had been wounded and taken prisoner at Shiloh, was later released, and after rejoining the Army was wounded – nearly fatally – at the fall of Atlanta.

On April 15, he wrote his wife: "I write you tonight with a heavy heart. As you must surely know by this time our beloved President was cruelly assassinated last night … I was in the theater… The events of the sad evening are a blur in my mind."

General Hedrick became editor and half owner of the *Ottumwa Courier* in 1866. In 1870 he was appointed supervisor of Internal Revenue for Iowa, Nebraska, Minnesota, Colorado and Dakota, a post which he held until 1876. Upon retiring from the newspaper, he devoted his time to the interests of the Cedar Rapids, Sigourney and Ottumwa Railroad Co., of which he was president. He was held in high esteem in this area, and the town of Hedrick was named in his honor.

Major Samuel Mahon of Ottumwa was in Washington D.C. as General Sherman's Army of the Tennessee marched in review on May 24, 1865. He was elected as 1st Lt. of Co. F of the 7th Regiment of the Iowa Volunteer Infantry at the age of twenty, after the regiment was mustered July 24, 1861. He was mustered out with the rank of major on July 14, 1865. He wrote the following, in part, to his sister of the May 24 review: "Most of the general officers had wreaths thrown over their horses. General Sherman and Logan were literally covered with them. Even your humble servant, as he moved in grand ovation on his prancing steed, received the affectionate regards of some damsel in the shape of a bouquet, which he tied to his saber."

Always known after the war as Major Mahon, he returned to Ottumwa and was in the successful wholesale grocery business with J.H. Merrill. The company was known as J.H. Merrill & Co. until 1915, the year of Mahon's death, when the name was changed to Samuel Mahon Co.

As Major Mahon passed in review with Sherman's army, the widow of Abraham Lincoln lay prostrate in a darkened White House surrounded by straw to muffle the sound of traffic. She never recovered. Major Rathbone and his fiancé, Clara, married and later moved to Germany, where he died in a mental institution after stabbing and then shooting her to death.

John Wilkes Booth was shot through the neck after a twelve-day manhunt. The shot paralyzed him, leaving him to die in agony the next morning. The last words on his lips, not uttered in Latin, were, "Useless. Useless."

Days Gone By

JARRETT GARNER'S MEMORIES

All of us wish that, with a blink of an eye and a click of the heels, we could transport ourselves back in time through our own time machine. But, alas, this is left to fantasy, and being earthbound, we search through documents and photographs to the time where our "blinks" and "clicks" are unable to take us.

On March 17, 1936 Jarrett W. Garner, at the age of ninety, one of Ottumwa's most successful businessmen, became our time machine, and wrote of his memories of early Ottumwa. He and his parents came here from Burlington in 1858 when he was nine. They traveled from Burlington to the end of the railroad line at Fairfield, and from there came by spring wagon to Ottumwa. This was the family's second move, as they came from Ohio to Burlington when Mr. Garner was three.

As happened with many families moving west, the Garners followed other family members to Ottumwa and moved in with relatives in a home at the corner of Green and Fifth Streets. Now known as 232 East Fifth Street, the house stood on the bluff "where the back porch looked down over the woods and the little town of Ottumwa, then a population of about one thousand."

Awakened from his first night's sleep here by someone calling "Over," he was told that the ferry was being called to cross the river and pick someone up on the other side, as there were no bridges. One could cross, however, at Market Street by horse and buggy "when the river was within its banks." As for the other side of the river, he recalls "there were no buildings on the south side of the river; it was all woods."

Mr. Garner attended school three years in the basement of the Methodist Church, a stone building located on the site of the current courthouse parking lot. As a boy he sang soprano in the Methodist Church choir during the winter months. Also during those months, the church held well-attended revivals, which Mr. Garner believed to be quite entertaining, as he viewed one heavyset gentleman, who, with each revival, would start from the back of the church on his hands and knees and leap forward saying "Amen" with each leap. (This should bring a smile to the most dour under any circumstances!)

After these services, the young men would line up in rows outside the church and ask to escort the young ladies home. And, as the church was the central focus in most of the lives of the day, while attending a social at the First Congregational Church, then located on the southwest corner of Third and Court Streets, he met "a charming young lady" who would become his wife.

As he gives us a further glimpse into the social life of a young boy during the Civil War era in Ottumwa, he recalls a "fancy dress party" held west of town attended by both boys and girls, to which he went dressed as a Zouave (a member of a French infantry unit composed of Algerians wearing brilliant uniforms) while some of the others dressed as a Highlander, a sailor, a military officer and a Turk. Other memories include tallow candles and the pony at his disposal from an uncle who owned a livery stable.

We agree with Mr. Garner when he states that "Memory is a wonderful thing," and today, as we read what he set down in 1936, we are very grateful that "these – are very vivid in my mind."

Michael W. Lemberger

The house at 232 East Fifth Street where Jarrett Garner heard calls for the Des Moines River Ferry, before the first bridge was built. Photo taken in 2007.

Days Gone By

IN SPITE OF JACK FROST

During the winter months, long before television, radio and electric lights, the streams and rivers afforded hours of entertainment on the ice even after nightfall with lanterns, candles, bonfires or a romantic full moon for the courting lovers. Back in those days one could step directly from the riverbank onto the ice and be ready to play "Crack the Whip" at a moment's notice.

It is easy to assume that everyone in that day and age would have a modicum of proficiency, at least, for ice skating, but an 1860 account of a misadventure on ice denies this assumption. In the words of a very disgruntled novice of that skill, it is reported, "We have got through skating. It's humbug. It's a vexation of spirit, of business, of flesh, and a tearer of trousers. It's a head-bumping, back-aching, leg wearing institution, and we warn people against skating. We tried it and shant be able to walk for a month...."

So, there it is. Not everyone glided with pleasure up the Des Moines River to Eddyville or down the river to Eldon.

Lemberger collection

Gone, also, are the days when snowballs flew at sleighs and bobsleds from new-fallen snow while boys ran after them to hitch a ride. The only light that could be seen came from the twinkling Milky Way as sleigh bells sang to the melody of laughter from numerous sledding parties on the hills. Sliding down any hill in the city would take these adventurers straight to the river with three slides being the maximum due to the long walk back up. So the hills, which were the dread of many teamsters, became flying carpets of winter fun.

There were dangers on the prairie for winter rides though, one being perpetrated by pranksters, the other by Old Man Winter. Nearing a high snow drift, the daring pranksters would overturn the bobsled—a wagon with runners attached in winter—to embarrass the fair maidens, enabling the so called "gentlemen" glimpses of forbidden ankles, gaiters and petticoats beneath the upended skirts! All would gather around and right the sled up and then go merrily on their way.

The other danger was far more serious, with unexpected snowstorms sweeping in, or as in the case of two groups who started out from Oskaloosa for Kirkville in 1867 and became lost. With the snow being 12 to 14 inches deep, they soon were overwhelmed, with everything covered by the depth of the snow. It took one group four hours to go the thirteen miles to Kirkville while the other group found themselves in Eddyville after five hours!

Whether the entertainment was skating, sledding down hills or riding in sleighs and bobsleds bundled in straw, blankets and robes, the refreshments afterwards were certain to include one or all of the following: Hot chocolate, cookies, popcorn, apples, doughnuts or cake. This is as true today as it was those many days ago, though there are no sledding parties down Ottumwa's hills or skating by stepping onto the frozen river from the banks of downtown. In fact, this entertainment enjoyed by so many in the days gone by, are shared today by very few. Few are the horses and sleighs, with ice skating available year round in indoor rinks as trains, planes and automobiles become the flying carpets to take us to far away places for our winter fun.

Days Gone By

MEN AND THEIR VEHICLES

Just as men take pride in their vehicles today, they also did so in the past, though the vehicles of the past had four legs instead of four wheels. Philo T. Overman, brother of Richmond ferry operator John Overman, recalled how important horse racing was – it "was the popular pioneer sport." It was the NASCAR and drag racing of the century.

According to Overman, there were a number of circular tracks, but the favorite tracks were on the straightaways, the most popular being a lane a quarter mile long between what is now Church Street and the river, lined by zigzag rail fences. It was nearly opposite the site where St. Patrick's Church would later be erected.

The fence, on both sides of the lane, made a perfect position for bystanders, and Overman recounts a particular race between two men named Jim Hunt and Ed Wiatt, who were particularly proud of their "vehicles." A race between the two was finally arranged, with the horses at stake.

The day of the race arrived, and speeding down the lane they came. Hunt won the race by a nose length, but Wiatt kept right on going and did not stop until he reached his home near Ormanville. The winner of the race lost his prize – no doubt Wiatt had his escape planned for this eventuality!

A horse race we would all have liked to have seen did not take place in Iowa, but in the southwest between a decrepit-looking, knock-kneed Apache Indian pony and a sleek cavalry mount. It was not unusual for the Indians and the cavalry horses to have races when tensions were at ease.

Lemberger collection

Harness racing at the Wapello County Fairgrounds, when it was located on Mary Street.

Sue Parrish

Civil War Col. Richard Irving Dodge, aide-de-camp to General Sherman, relates the tale of the cavalry mount, who was known for its speed, being challenged by the Indians in his book *Our Wild Indians,* published in 1883. When the appointed time for the race arrived, the Apaches brought forward the most disreputable Indian pony one could imagine, and with laughs and snickers, the entire command bet on the cavalry horse.

What occurred next defied the logic of any experienced horse breeder, and would certainly be a classic for the funniest video of today. When the flag was dropped, the Apache mounted his pony backwards and took off, making faces and gestures at the crowd as his pony left the cavalry steed in the dust. What was not known by the bettors was that this Indian pony was a legend throughout the west for its speed!

Col. Dodge did not believe the reservation system was in the best interest of anyone, most of all the Native Americans.

Lemberger collection

Days Gone By

CASTER'S FLATS:
Confusing Two Buildings

When the original structure at 913 East Main Street was built as a hospital in 1871 by Dr. Paul Caster, a "magnetic healer" who had not attended medical school, little did anyone know that many years later it would become known as Caster's Flats and be confused with another building three blocks away, which would also be known as Caster's Flats.

Dr. Caster's building, known as the Caster House Medical Infirmary, attracted patients from miles around for his magnetic healing, achieved by stimulating the subconscious mind to heal the body through the massaging of muscles and manipulation of bones. This form of medicine was widely used across the United States at the time, with Dr. Caster becoming one of the more successful practitioners. Pictures appeared of him surrounded by large numbers of crutches and contraptions no longer needed by those whom he had healed. He soon had to add to his original building. An addition was completed in 1875, and another wing containing his home was added in 1878.

Dr. Caster died in 1881, eleven days before his 54th birthday. It is unclear what the building was used for in the next few years. In 1885, Dr. D. A. LaForce, a former surgeon in the Union Army and practicing physician in Agency for fourteen years, purchased it and renamed it Hawkeye Hospital, going into business with his two physician sons.

In 1892 the Ottumwa Hospital Association was formed, and in July 1894 the association rented Dr. Caster's residence from Dr. LaForce and opened their hospital. In June 1898, Dr. LaForce approached the Ottumwa Hospital Association with a proposal to merge the two hospitals. With this being done, the Ottumwa Hospital took over the Hawkeye Hospital until a new hospital building was completed in 1905 at the corner of East Second and College Streets. When the Ottumwa Hospital building—known as the hospital across form the high school—was razed in 1971, it stepped into history and is remembered as a grand old lady with its dignity intact. Not so with Caster House Medical Infirmary, a.k.a. Hawkeye Hospital, a.k.a. Ottumwa Hospital, a.k.a. The Glendon, a.k.a. Caster's Flats.

When the Ottumwa Hospital opened in 1905 on East Second Street, Caster's

Lemberger collection

Built in the 1870s by Dr. Paul Caster as a hospital, this building was later known as the Glendon and then as Caster Flats. It was torn down in 1983.

infirmary, which had begun as a center for healing and was visited by hundreds, began a steady decline as an apartment complex not known for any amenities. It was finally condemned by the city when the original portion was 113 years old.

Confusion arises with another structure, also known as Caster's Flats, which was featured in the late 1930s in *Ripley's Believe It or Not*. This structure was said to be the only three-story building in the United States which could be entered from three streets and had no stairs. Given Ottumwa's topography and street configuration, this was not an impossibility, and it will always be remembered as the building with many levels which could be entered from East Second Street, Birch Street, and Vine Street.

Both complexes had seen a lot of living. When the multi-street entrance "Caster's Flats" gasped its last breath under attack by the city's wrecking crews, bystanders will swear that "cockroaches as large as horses" scurried for cover. Both structures will remain known as Caster's Flats in the legends of Ottumwa, and will also remain as causes for a small amount of confusion.

Days Gone By

CIGARS, BICYCLES and CAMERAS

John A., William H., and Thomas A. Pallister were born in Canada and came to Ottumwa with their parents in 1872. John A. opened a confectionery and ice cream store on East Main Street, and eleven years later the brothers were in business together as Pallister Brothers at 220 East Main Street.

Securely established, the brothers received a franchise to sell the Columbia bicycle. With amateur photography on the rise, they also received a franchise for the Eastman Kodak camera. The entrepreneurs were off and running full speed ahead. They added cigar and cigar box manufacturing to the confectionery business in 1889, as the selling of cigars was a part of the confectionery and ice cream business during that time.

By 1890, when the Coal Palace opened in September, they not only exhibited their line of cigars, but they had a two light Weston machine on display, the first electric light machine in Ottumwa, which they used to light their store.

John Pallister had introduced the high-wheeled bicycle to Ottumwa, but it soon disappeared with the introduction of the chain drive, which allowed for wheels of equal size. In 1888 the pneumatic tire was invented, which greatly improved not only the ride, but the ability to handle the bicycle. The Pallister Brothers introduced this chain-driven Columbia bicycle to the area, and with their Kodak camera and cigar manufacturing, they became known all over southern Iowa.

Each brother managed a separate part of the business: Tom, cigar manufacturing; William, confectionery and ice cream; John, bicycle and camera. Both were businesses in which John excelled by becoming a champion bicyclist and expert photographer.

During the 1890's Ottumwa became the bicycle-racing capital of the United States. John Pallister was one of the racing stars in the country, achieving his fame originally on

Lemberger collection

70

the high-wheeler. In 1886 Frank B. Thrall joined the League of American Wheelmen and became their Iowa representative in 1887. Due to the influence of Frank Thrall and John Pallister, as a champion racer, it was not difficult for Ottumwa to accomplish that achievement of being the racing capital. Around 1890 the Kite Track on Mary Street began holding the races, but in 1897 Ottumwa finished a bicycle track on West Second Street, which was regarded as the fastest track in the world. National contests

Lemberger collection

were held here, with world records established among 400 competitors.

The 1890s were the glory days for bicycle racing. Interest began to wane around the turn of the 20th century and this track, which had cost $12,000 to build, was soon closed and taken over by the Mississippi Valley League Baseball with that game on its way to becoming "America's pass time."

John A. Pallister's fastest one hundred mile race from start to finish was completed in eight hours and fifty-four minutes. He retired to Denver, Colorado. He returned for his brother William's funeral in May, 1927, but was taken ill and died three weeks later in the Ottumwa Hospital.

These were three Ottumwans — children of an English father and a Canadian mother — who contributed to putting Ottumwa on the map, provided employment, and would have been very interesting to know.

Days Gone By

LITTLE LADY FROM GENOA

It is hard to imagine the cosmopolitan flavor of this community during the latter quarter of the 19th century and into the early 20th century, as immigrants from all over Europe converged on this prairie town to better their lives, bringing with them the multitude of trades from their unique cultures needed for the growth of the area. Combined with the different accents which developed while learning English, it was a community whose nuances we shall only know through our imaginations. With these immigrants came talents which contributed to them finding the American Dream.

Such is the story of a little lady born in Genoa, Italy.

Mrs. Columbia Celania emigrated to the United States in 1870. After living in Chicago for a number of years, she and her husband, Ludwig, moved to Omaha, where Ludwig died, leaving her with five children. Arriving in Ottumwa shortly after her husband's death, with the five children to support — four boys and one girl — and $500 in hand, she opened a candy and ice cream store in 1890 at 325 East Main Street, at a time when most businesswomen were confined to dressmaking and millinery.

Longdo collection

Longdo collection

Celania Brothers Ice Cream store, about 1911

Making candy on a cook stove and ice cream with a hand-operated freezer, her business produced ten gallons of ice cream per day. It is not hard to believe it was a family affair to accomplish an output of ten gallons of ice cream per day with a hand operated freezer.

Soon fruit was added, and Columbia had a thriving fruit and confectionery business requiring a move to 307-309 East Main Street. The business eventually produced one thousand gallons of ice cream per day to be shipped all over Iowa and beyond. It is not hard to believe, being Italian, that she produced what was to become an American favorite: Neapolitan — chocolate, vanilla and strawberry ice cream side by side — which originated in her homeland and was introduced into the United States in the 1870s.

Mrs. Celania suffered from Bright's disease and passed away at the age of fifty-eight, on September 8, 1905. Three of her sons, Charles, Joe and Tony, took over the business, and it became known as Celania Bros., a business still remembered by Ottumwa natives today. Ironically, Tony also died at the age of fifty-eight, in January, 1935, leaving his two brothers to operate the business.

Mrs. Celania, through her business acumen and hard work, provided for her family while leaving them a legacy, as her strong Roman Catholic faith empowered her through her deepest valleys.

Days Gone By

THE GREAT APHRODISIAC

Man has always had a craving for sweets, with cavemen gathering honey to satisfy this hunger. Middle Eastern countries made delectable delights from honey, adding fruit and nuts, but it was during the Middle Ages that sugar and water replaced honey — for the very wealthy only, as the cost of sugar was prohibitive.

By the 19th century, however, America had candy makers in the back of their general stores and special confectionery shops shipping out penny candies to an insatiable market. It was the advancement in automated machinery that took candymaking out of the back room of a store into large factories, and Walter T. Hall & Co. of Ottumwa, founded in 1880, was one of these.

It was an Irishman, John Hanam, who with a Mr. Baker, opened America's first chocolate mill — Baker's Chocolate — in 1780 in Dorchester, Massachusetts, importing the cocoa beans from the West Indies. Western Europe had begun a love affair with chocolate centuries before, not long after the Spanish were introduced to it by the Mayans. Chocolate soon became a favorite, with new methods of candy manufacturing, and Ottumwa became a center.

The Walter T. Hall & Co. located at the intersection of Third and Market Streets, became the largest producer of candy west of Chicago, and small wonder. Mr. Hall, intuitively believing chocolate was what consumers would ultimately enjoy in candy, became a pioneer in the field, and chocolate candy became Hall's specialty. It was a real craft to hand-dip chocolates before the advent of the dipping machine. Hand-dipped chocolates were shipped nationwide, and in the three-story factory, the candy maker made confections no other company produced, with some cookers putting out 8,000 pounds per day.

It is a testament to Hall's products and his business acumen that the business survived the economic instabilities and panics of the 19th and early 20th centuries, as well as World War I and the Great Depression. Out of more than 20 candy factories in Iowa at the onset of the depression of the 1930's, Walter T. Hall & Co. was the only candy factory in Iowa to survive, producing chocolates and other taste teasers until closing its doors in 1957.

Sue Parrish

It was a foreman of the company, Frank Petrovic, a naturalized U.S. citizen born in Czechoslovakia, who invented the peanut-cluster making machine that put new meaning into the Hall motto, "Tease the Taste." The machine was patented July 8, 1941, and peanut clusters rolled off the line at the factory at the corner of Third and Market, to be shipped nationwide in gallon buckets. The peanut cluster was born!

Few, if any, remember the Tower-Majors Candy Company located on South Jefferson Street, known as the "House of Chocolates" with their Perfection Chocolates. Begun in 1905 by James Majors and C. R. Tower, the House of Chocolates was no match for Tease the Taste, and was out of business before 1925.

Sugar and chocolate have become a staple for most Americans, good or bad.

Longdo collection

Walter T. Hall Company, manufacturer of chocolates, was located at the intersection of Third and Market Streets.

Days Gone By

THE STAFF OF LIFE

Butcher, baker and candlestick maker. Well, we certainly had butchers and bakers, but the candlestick makers?

Before there was a nearby flour mill, the first settlers had to go miles to mills to have their grain ground, and then would have to wait in line for their turn. Sometimes these ventures could take up to two weeks, and after returning, flour would be shared with neighbors who had none. Some resorted to grinding flour in coffee mills or manually with grinding stones as the Indians did. But, from wherever the flour came, the end result was the same: The wonderful smell of baking bread to whet the appetite.

Later, most communities, Ottumwa included, had their small bake shops which later gave way to larger, more productive enterprises with the advancement in equipment. When Anton and Chris Lowenberg opened their bakery on South Court Street in 1875, they were on the cusp of a bread revolution: The meeting of the invention of the reaper, enabling the quick harvesting of wheat, with the rapid growth of railroads, encouraging western industrial growth. And it did not take long for the pervasive aroma from the ovens, combined with the high quality of their product, for them to have a burgeoning business from all walks of life.

The Lowenberg brothers were progressive businessmen and took quick advantage of advances within their profession. The merchandising trend within the industry was for bakeries to become identified with names. In 1904 Anton's young son, Art, suggested they name their product "Mary Jane" after the girlfriend of the comic strip character "Buster Brown." It was agreed upon, and the name Lowenberg Bakery became synonymous with Mary Jane and later with Sunbeam Bread.

After Lowenberg's, other bakeries opened in the city, including C.H. Smith Bakery, Range Bakery, Iowa Baking Company, Ottumwa Bake-Rite Bakery, South Side Bakery, and Dupy's Bakery. While Dupy's and Lowenberg's survived through succeeding generations, the others could not compete and fell by the wayside.

All remember the Swenson Bakery, but it actually was not opened until the middle

Longdo collection

Lowenberg Bakery's "new" facility on West Second Street, built in 1923. This photograph was taken some years later.

of the 20th century and it would be considered a bake shop for specialty items. Swensons – and Dupy's in later years – was a spot where you could drop in while shopping and order your favorite roll or long john as you lingered over coffee to rest tired feet.

When the ovens at Lowenberg's were "full steam ahead," the whole community was wrapped within a king-sized blanket of olfactory delight, giving a sense that all was right with the world. It was a dark day in 1984 when the last oven cooled down, taking with it that reassuring aroma of the "staff of life" that daily drifted across the community for 109 years – inspiring the imagination to the inevitable slathering of the warm slices with rich butter and favorite jam. As the aroma slipped into memory, the community was left with a loss which still lingers, as the old building at Second and Wapello Streets gave way to a new structure for our law enforcement center.

Days Gone By

THE EGG LADY

When Ottumwa became the largest exporter of eggs and butter in Iowa, and later had the honor of being the largest shipping point in the United States for these products, it wasn't the farm women or the women with a chicken house and cow "out back" who were recognized for this contribution to our economy.

In the agricultural economy of the 19th century and into the 20th century, women were responsible for the maintenance of the home, including household expenses and clothing, through the sale of eggs and butter. Many women saved their families from total destitution during hard times through this endeavor. It was part of the culture of the farm and an accepted fact of life.

After railroad growth exploded with the end of the Civil War, Ottumwa, due to its location near the central point of the United States, quickly became a railroad hub. With this came the industrialists and the entrepreneurs to take advantage of our raw materials, and the sale of butter and eggs quickly found markets as far away as San Francisco, as testified to in the June 21, 1869 issue of the *San Francisco Chronicle* with the headline, "Eggs and Butter from Iowa: The First Overland Importation."

The article reads as follows: "A gentleman doing business in this city yesterday received three boxes containing 140 dozen eggs, and six boxes containing 325 pounds of butter, which were consigned to him from Ottumwa, Iowa, and came through in eleven days via the Pacific railroad. The butter, tho' not so rich in flavor or as fine in color as good California made, is very fair and sold readily at 35 cents per pound. The eggs were taken in a single lot at 42 ½ cents per dozen and we shall probably see 'Iowa egg nog' labels in some of the saloons and 'Iowa Omelet' at some of the restaurants. The world seems to move — about this time, when Iowa eggs and butter, fresh and sweet, form a part of the food supply of San Francisco."

Taking advantage of the eggs and butter economy in Ottumwa, Samuel Lilburn of St. Louis opened a shipping and distribution business, Samuel Lilburn & Co., in 1872 with cold storage buildings at the corner of Second and Green Streets. He soon became known as the "The Butter King of the West," with suppliers not only in Iowa, but Kansas, Missouri, Nebraska and Illinois shipping to Lilburn's, who, in turn from

The Samuel Lilburn building, located at East Second and Green Streets. The building later became the home of the local Benevolent and Protective Order of Elks.

this railroad hub sent the produce to the large American markets of Philadelphia, New York, and Boston as well as San Francisco. Not to stop there, smaller markets were reached across the United States from Washington to Maine including Texas. By 1893, two million pounds of butter and two million dozen eggs a year left Ottumwa's shipping yards.

Mr. Lilburn passed away in 1888, having turned his business over in 1887 to A.W. Johnson. The business was better known, after Mr. Lilburn's death, under the direction of John B. Dennis, who purchased his interest in 1889.

Gone are the days of fried chicken dinners or chicken and noodles with the meat from a plump hen prepared by the lady of the house from the fruits of her labors. Good home grown "fryers" are short in supply, too, as well as those who know how to "turn" them! They left with the "egg lady," who, just a blink of an eye ago, delivered her farm-fresh eggs to the town homemaker and the grocery store on the corner.

Days Gone By

CRATES AND CANDY

One hundred years ago, back in the days when our city dwelling ancestors were bustling about preparing for Christmas, it was the heyday of the fruit, vegetable and wholesale grocers. This was also the heyday of the hard candy that only came out at Christmas. The chocolates came from Hall's Candy Co. and had to either have a fast turnover or kept cool, as preservatives were not in use. The art of the well trimmed window, as building an attractive, eye catching display from perishables and canned goods, taxed the patience and ingenuity of the most talented.

There was fierce competition on South Court Street, where the majority of downtown grocers operated, until the modern food store chains gradually put them and the neighborhood corner grocer out of business. Preparing for Christmas was as much, if not more, of a major event for local grocers and meat markets as it was for the other merchants. With their businesses decorated, their products were proudly displayed with hanging plucked turkeys, geese and ducks, every kind of roast as well as sausage, pork and fish, all out for inspection -- the "health dragons" had not been invented yet! It would be hard to miss the prominent red heart of Morrell "Iowa's Pride" hams prominently displayed on display shelves as customers entered the stores.

Grocers made certain specialty items were ordered in proper quantity and regular items were well-stocked. In order to fill all wants, orders were solicited from customers, as the telephone was still a luxury in many homes. The sleigh was made ready for deliveries if the weather warranted. This was also the day of pecans and walnuts arriving at Christmas time by bulk in barrels; un-waxed apples ready for the "sleeve" to bring out that bright, red shine, and the ever-present grocer's cat on constant rodent control.

Crates of Christmas oranges were ordered through the wholesale fruit and vegetables houses of Lagomarcino-Grupe Co., John I. Finnerty or E. H. Emery & Co. Bananas were available year round, being purchased by the grocer on the stalk and cut off to suit the customers' needs while watching for that sometime tarantula in hiding.

The wholesale grocers of J. G. Hutchison & Co. and J. H. Merrill Co. could be depended on for the other grocery needs with their salesmen in constant contact with retail grocers. John Morrell & Co. supplied most of the meat, though Swift Co. was in operation in Ottumwa. Poultry, eggs and butter wholesaled through the John B. Dennis Co. and others, including Burnaugh Produce Co. at 711 Church Street. and Iowa Produce Co. on South Union Street near Swift Co.

There is no doubt that the holiday seasons of years ago were events looked forward to with gratitude and hope-filled anticipation. Today we have turned them upside-down, as many of us have made them into stress-filled, exhausting events, unknown in the past.

A.P. Anderson Grocery during the 1890s.

PROPRIETRESS OF DRY GOODS

1890 was a very important year for Ottumwa, as new businesses were springing up and the Ottumwa Coal Palace was preparing to open to celebrate southern Iowa's growth and industry. In February of that year, the same year Columbia Celania opened her ice cream and confectionery business, Sarah Cullen, known as Sadie, the former manager of the retail store Israel Bros., founded the S.C. Cullen & Company with a partner, B.A. Warner. This move opened the way for Ms. Cullen to become one of the most successful businesswomen in Iowa.

She was born in Ottumwa in 1859, one of 12 children born to building contractor James Cullen and his wife, Sarah O'Conner Cullen. Sadie's father was responsible for many commercial construction projects in the area including St. Mary of the Visitation, known as old St. Mary's, built in 1860-1861.

Located at 126-130 East Main Street, Sadie's business was the only one in Ottumwa dealing strictly in ladies' dry goods, and it took little time for her business to take the lead. S.C. Cullen & Company became the largest dry goods store in the area, which led to her business becoming known statewide. This was quite an accomplishment for a single woman in a business climate of burgeoning industrialism and stiff competition.

A number of factors contributed to her success, along with her brother, Tom, who was in charge of advertising. One factor was her acute perception of what was desired by her customers in fabrics and trimmings, culminating in her buying trips to New York twice a year to purchase fashionable merchandise. She retailed this quality merchandise at low prices while exercising unique and appealing window and store displays. The courtesy extended to customers by all store personnel won the business permanent allegiance.

In 1893, Mr. Warner relinquished his interest. In 1899 the forty-year-old businesswoman married E. P. Barton, a Philadelphian in the dry goods business, who managed the firm after their marriage. Sadie died childless in 1918 at the age of fifty-nine. The business closed in 1928 and Mr. Barton passed away in 1931. The building at 126 East Main Street was known as the "Barton Building" until that block was demolished during urban renewal.

S. C. CULLEN & CO.

DEALERS IN

Fine Dress Goods,

SILKS AND CLOAKS,

Hosiery, Underwear, Corsets,

LINENS,

Laces,   Domestics,

The Ottumwa Store,

128-130 -- Main St. -- 128-130

BLAKE'S SISTER, MARY

Among Ottumwa's earlier settlers was Charles F. Blake, who was born in Prussia October 12, 1823. At the age of twenty-two he came to Ottumwa with members of his family, including his younger sister, Mary, also born in Prussia on January 16, 1826. The family had immigrated to the United States in 1836, settling in Ohio and Indiana for a short time before setting their roots down in Ottumwa.

Charles Blake was involved in real estate, among other endeavors, and hit the California gold fields for three years before returning to Ottumwa in 1853. He went into the pharmaceutical business in 1865 under the name of Taylor, Blake & Co., a business which later evolved into the Edgerly Wholesale Pharmaceutical Co. His fingers were in touch with all of Ottumwa's growth, from the railroad industry to banking. He was one of the first stockholders and directors of the Iowa National Bank, with Dr. James L. Taylor. In 1873, Blake was elected the bank's president.

What about his sister, Mary?

Mary became the bride of one of Ottumwa's noted earliest settlers, Newton C. Hill. Hill, who was five years older than Mary, had been born in North Carolina, and was a carpenter by trade. The two became one in October, 1847 and set about raising a family, which would eventually include nine children, while he practiced his trade in the growing hamlet. In 1855 N. C. Hill became Ottumwa's treasurer, a position his brother-in-law, Charles Blake, also held at one time.

Dr. Taylor was interested in stock raising and farming and perhaps, though it's only a speculation, he and Hill's brother-in-law, Charles Blake, induced Hill to give up carpentry and go into farming and stock raising. Whatever the motive, N.C. Hill did go into agriculture by developing Oakland Farm. He built a sturdy brick home for Mary and his children, as he became the breeder of shorthorn cattle. They lived in this home until 1892 when they moved to Highland Center to be cared for by a son, Charles, where Mary preceded her husband in death on April 10, 1899.

Obituaries can be confusing bits of information, and may not always be accurate. This is the case for Mary's: One obituary, in *The Courier* of April 13, states that her service was held from the Methodist Episcopal Church of Highland Center "yesterday," but a separate obituary, dated the same day, states through information given to *The Courier* by her daughter Mrs. H.L. Waterman, "who was present at the time of her death," that "tomorrow" the service will be held. The *Courier* issued the following statement in the same Waterman article: "The funeral will be held from the late residence at 9:30 o'clock Wednesday morning."

Where the service was held and when is not clear, and no one alive today attended to give us the particulars, but one thing is certain: The farm was "eaten up" by urban sprawl years ago, leaving the brick home N.C. Hill built for his family still standing in Section 18 of Center Township, on the corner of North Court Street and East Manning Avenue, just two blocks from his namesake, Hill Avenue.

Michael W. Lemberger

Newton and Mary Hill's house at North Court Street and East Manning Avenue, as it looked in 2007.

THE ART OF ENTERTAINING

In western culture during the waning years of Queen Victoria's reign, the art of entertaining reached its pinnacle. Maybe Ottumwa didn't hit the stride of Mrs. Cornelius Vanderbilt, but a good time was assured by gracious hosts and hostesses no matter their pecuniary circumstances. These evenings of entertainment, supplemented with available culinary delights, were achieved in theme-based settings.

Mr. and Mrs. J. W. Garner began 1891 with an evening of entertainment in their home at 424 East Second Street — the site is now a parking lot for Wesley United Methodist Church — and ended that year with an evening's entertainment for the thirty-member boys' choir of St. Mary's Episcopal Church.

The event at the Garner home in January, 1891 was in celebration of England's Poet Laureate, Alfred Lord Tennyson. The entertainment began with an instrumental selection from the works of Chopin performed by Miss Marguerite Walker. This was followed by a review of the life and works of the poet by Miss Alice Rogers. The entertainment continued throughout the evening with vocal and instrumental solos and recitations with the two parlors and music room open and filled with chrysanthemums and carnations. It is recorded that the interpretation of the death scene from the love story of Lancelot and Elaine, as recited by Mrs. J. B. Sax, "would never be forgotten."

When the wholesale dry goods merchant and his wife entertained the boys' choir from their church in December, games were played followed by a supper of turkey and sandwiches, fruitcake and cream. At their 10:00 p.m. departure, each boy was given the choice of a rose or carnation boutonniere.

In the home of Miss Mary Dixon on East Court Street, The Forty Club met on December 7, 1891. "Beautiful white and red chrysanthemums made the rooms fragrant, which together with handsome draperies and appointments made a pleasing effect upon the eyes." The game of Drive Whist entertained the club, with winners given pieces of hand-painted Haviland china as prizes.

"A most delightful evening of pleasure was enjoyed, wit and merriment ruling the hour," when Miss Maggie Workman entertained four tables of High Five players on December 9, serving them refreshments of tropical fruits and cake after passing out prizes.

Sue Parrish

On December 11, the forty-five attendants of a surprise 18th-birthday party for Maggie Gilmore danced in masquerade costumes to an orchestra until the wee hours of the morning.

While these social events were recorded, may others of the same kind went unrecorded. Rest assured, everyone who opened their home to guests for an evening's entertainment during those golden years used their best of everything, as decorum mattered up and down the social scale, with dining tables devoid of elbows and seated males wearing caps or hats!

"Hope smiles on the year to come, whispering that it will be happier...."
-- Alfred Lord Tennyson

Longdo collection

A typical upper-class Victorian home

Days Gone By

THE VILLAGE ON THE OTHER SIDE

Our first glimpse of South Ottumwa is through the eyes of A.W. Rankin, a resident of Davis County, who in 1901 set down what he recalled seeing as a young boy.

While on a trip with five men in March, 1841, they endeavored to visit Chief Keokuk's camp site at what is now Ottumwa's south side, located a mile from the river, which prevented enemy attack from under cover of the river bank.

He relates, "Many of the houses of this village had an upper story, reached by steps or notches cut in logs or poles, and all of the houses were covered with bark peeled from trees in such an ingenious manner that we soon learned to imitate their example and cover our own houses and porches in the same way."

Rankin noted that Keokuk was not in the village when they visited, but that he believed Hard Fish was there. He goes on to describe them as "all copper-colored, high cheek-boned with little or no beard and with little hair on the head, straight and rather tall." He continues that they "had little to say to us, and were stoical and indifferent to passing events." Though the warriors were outfitted with flintlock rifles, bows and arrows, tomahawks, scalping knives, and were as well armed "as any tribe in the Mississippi Valley," the whites had no fear of them.

As they continued through the village, the filth and dirt "in the extreme" of their food, as well as the "greasy and dirty trade blankets worn by men and women alike", stuck in his mind. He felt pity for the women, who performed all of the work while "nearly all these Indians were lazy, dirty and filthy in camp and tramp, the men leading an easy, indolent life on foot or horseback."

The filth in this village, which he believed applied to all of the tribes of the Upper Mississippi Valley, differed from later experiences he had with the Sioux and to "those farther west," and, he added, "I will say that I have seen nearly all of the tribes of the central portion of America."

Rankin traveled through the village south to the burial grounds, which is believed to be in the area later called "Monkey Mountain." (Legend tells us that, at a much later date while a circus was camped in that area, the monkeys from the circus escaped.) In this burial ground, all burials were underground with the deeds of the departed depicted through the paintings on the slabs of perishable wood, which he estimated could not have lasted more than twenty years. So in the area of "Monkey Mountain" – the current site of 194th Avenue, outside of the southeastern Ottumwa city limits – lie the remains of those left behind when Keokuk left Iowa.

In 1901 Mr. Rankin asks this question while visiting South Ottumwa: "I stop to quench my thirst from the clear, cool water just from the well….is this water drained off those poor savages buried here in my day…?"

Lemberger collection

Chief Keokuk

Days Gone By

VILLAGE CHALLENGES

South Ottumwa has its own unique history. When D. P. Inskeep named his little hamlet Pickwick, across from the village of Ottumwa, he had no idea how prophetic the name would become.

A syndicate of eastern investors headed by R. S. Smith (and upon his death in 1876, by his son, Dr. D. B. Smith) purchased Pickwick from Mr. Inskeep, which included two hundred acres. They led the incoming inhabitants on adventures which, when viewed in retrospect from more than one hundred years later, become humorous. Most of the adventures stem from the naivete of these founders and the reaction of the north side business men to these "upstarts" who would dare compete with them. Thus they became a Pickwick Club, reminiscent of the club led by Charles Dickens' character, Samuel Pickwick, in *The Pickwick Papers,* and the adventures of the south siders today bring the same chuckles as do the adventures of Pickwick, Snodgrass, Winkle, Tupman, and the servant Weller in Dickens' novel.

At the time, however, the adventures on the south side of the Des Moines River were of the serious kind.

One of the first obstacles for South Ottumwa to overcome concerning north side Ottumwa was the erection of a new bridge to replace the existing wooden toll bridge. This was accomplished when the county voted, after defeating the measure in two elections, to erect a new bridge. However, the building of the new bridge was delayed two years, due to the influence of the stockholders of the toll bridge on the commissioners. The issue was finally resolved when, in the words of Dr. Smith, "The Lord, being on my side, a flood carried off the old bridge and they had to build in 1880."

The challenge continued when South Ottumwa petitioned the Ottumwa Water Company for utilities. The request was turned down, and it wasn't until South Ottumwa residents committed themselves to developing their own water company that Ottumwa Water Company agreed to run their lines.

But the water line negotiation was a "walk in the park" compared to events which began in 1884 and ended in 1886.

In 1884 South Ottumwans applied for a charter for the building of streetcar railways, but instead of them receiving a charter, it was given to those opposed to it – who then sat on the charter for two years rather than building.

An electric streetcar at the south end of the Market Street Bridge. Electric cars replaced the original horsedrawn trolley cars starting in 1889, not long after service was extended to South Ottumwa.

R. T. Shea eventually received funding from Dr. Smith to purchase the franchise, and the heat was on. With this, an injunction was issued by the north siders against the building of the railway system.

R. T. Shea, being the cat in the cat and mouse game, deftly avoided the injunction. He purchased the street cars, rails and ties out of state, and kept them sitting on railroad cars several miles out of town, waiting for the orders to be given to bring them in.

On the Saturday evening before the Monday the franchise was to expire, the "Pickwick Club," including women and children, banded together and laid the streetcar railway. Under cover of darkness, using lanterns, they constructed tracks while the unsuspecting north side businessmen snored away. The north siders arose on Sunday morning to see mule-drawn streetcars appear before their wondering eyes at the corner of Market and Main Streets.

This caused no small stir, and with crowds riding all day over this new two-mile track, the north siders could take no more. They endeavored to tear up the tracks, which were being safeguarded by the south siders. The sheriff averted disaster and sent the north siders home. So as Mr. Pickwick states, we are "ruminating on the strange mutability of human affairs."

IMPEDED VILLAGE GROWTH

In 1885, the approximately 35 legal residents of South Ottumwa began steps to incorporate the 200 platted acres of the little community. But lo and behold, just before the process was to be completed in 1886, the Ottumwa City Council annexed the 200 acres.

With the latest act of opposition from the north side fathers, Dr. W. B. Smith, who had carried on the development of South Ottumwa after the death of his father, R. S. Smith, sought an injunction against this annexation. Losing in the circuit court, Dr. Smith appealed. Unwilling to take their chances in superior court, the north side resorted to their usual tactics of duplicity shrouded in shenanigans, and when the case was to be presented to the higher court, it was found that all of the records held by the Recorder's Office had "taken wings and flown."

Dr. Smith decided not to fight this issue any longer and gave in. He paid his attorney's fees and pressed on to another larger matter—the ward system.

When South Ottumwa was annexed, it became part of one of Ottumwa's existing wards, but had no representation on the city council, resulting in the old "taxation without representation" problem. As Dr. Smith fought to have South Ottumwa represented by its own aldermen, he now had a friend on Ottumwa's city council, in Peter Ballingall. Though the battle was long and hard, Ballingall's political acumen overcame bitter objections of north Ottumwa's influential residents, and the new ward south of the river became Ottumwa's largest ward, being served by two aldermen.

Dr. Smith originally sold lots sized 66 feet by 132 feet for $75 each, from his 200 acres. Most of the sales were on contract, and reportedly he had to repossess only one.

By 1890, the lots were being sold for $500 to $600. A population explosion in the five years between 1885 and 1890 led to more than 200 houses being built in 1889 alone.

Brick store buildings were springing up and new businesses seemed to be opening every day, representing flour mills, planing and feed mills, opera houses, wagon shops, a steam laundry, screen factory and many other smaller businesses – proving that South Ottumwa could indeed have been the autonomous, thriving industrial and business community the north side had feared after the Smiths began development.

Sue Parrish

Dr. Smith raised $750 — giving $350 himself — for the Ottumwa Coal Palace and was elected to its 13-member board of directors. He served as chairman of the entertainment and reception committee while serving on the building and printing committees. It is a sad comment that Ottumwa businessmen fought so hard to prevent an independent South Ottumwa, as there is no doubt that two autonomous communities, separated by the river, could have successfully worked together, avoiding the resulting rancor and division. There is much truth in "still waters run deep."

Lemberger collection

SOUTH OTTUMWA:
Another Side of the Story

The events which occurred during South Ottumwa's early growth are recorded in Volume I of a two-volume edition of *History of Wapello County*, published in 1914, with Harrison L. Waterman, supervising editor, placing the best light on the situation.

He gave little hint of the animosity which occurred between the two sides of the river – reminiscent of the Hatfield and McCoy feud in the Appalachians, though without the bloodshed. It came close, though, and Waterman, as a resident of South Ottumwa, endeavored to make certain that all would be forgotten with a bit of revisionist history thrown in. Dr. D. B. Smith's frustration and exasperation can only be read between the lines in Waterman's genteel version of the events of South Ottumwa's growth and, then, as with all historical events, the real flavor is lost with time.

Waterman asserts that the builders of South Ottumwa "met with some opposition. There were some influential men north of the river who said, and apparently believed, that the building of what they called a rival town would be serious injury to the business interests of the City of Ottumwa, but the lapse of time has shown that these men were mistaken."

Lemberger collection

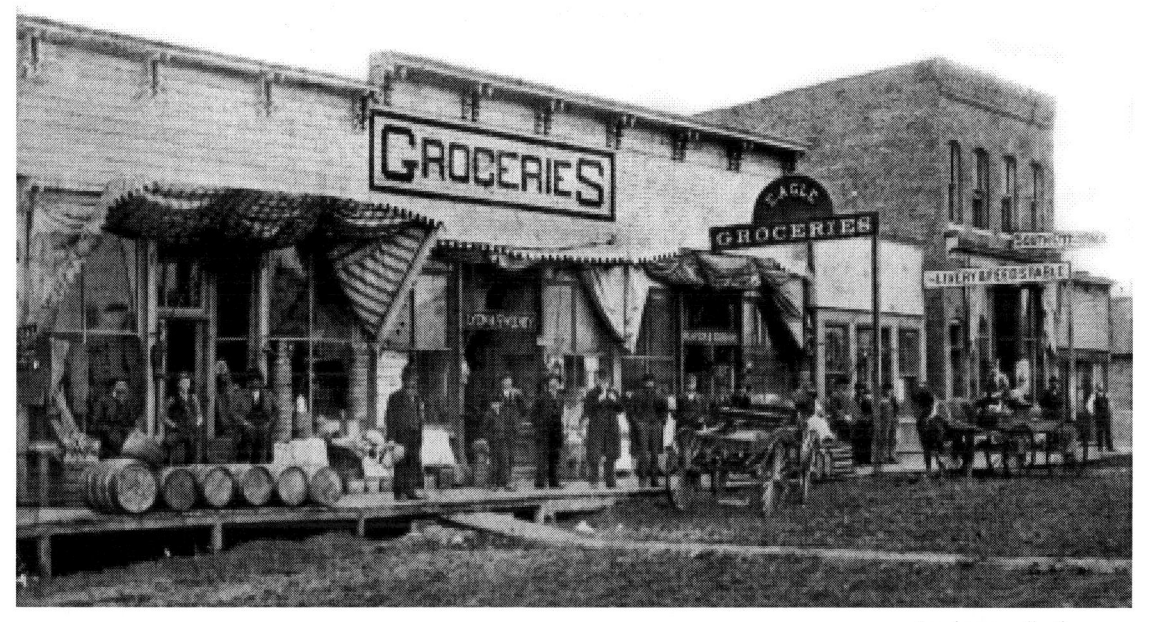

Lemberger collection

Mr. Waterman first viewed South Ottumwa on his way to the Bear Creek gold mines. It was 1881, before South Ottumwa had reached its boom time, and there appeared to be no drainage, with weeds in possession of the swampy town site with the "business end of the place ... down near the south end approach to the Market Street bridge." He, along with the others in his group, agreed that it would not grow any larger. But when he returned in 1887, it had taken on a totally different appearance with "every resident of the place" being "a hustler and a booster."

The "some opposition" thwarted every plan for improvements, and it was only when the South Ottumwa Boosters began to implement plans of their own for these improvements that the city of Ottumwa relented, faced with this competition. A newspaper — The *South Ottumwa News* — played a large part in the community receiving the improvements, as it constantly urged the inhabitants of that side of the river "to assert their rights and demand their portion of public improvements."

In 1914 Waterman states that "South Ottumwa, with its 8,000 population, is a part of the city, and all of our people feel an interest in the growth and prosperity of Ottumwa. The river now and always was an imaginary line." This statement could probably be debated, but Waterman goes on, "What is good for North Ottumwa is good for South Ottumwa and vice versa, and we feel we should all pull together."

As the wise teacher has written in the book of Ecclesiastes, "There is nothing new under the sun."

Days Gone By

SOUTH OTTUMWA'S GOLD RUSH

J. O. Briscoe, while grinding limestone in the Bear Creek area in 1881, asserted that he was finding gold and silver in the dust he was collecting. Nothing lights the fire in the bosom of man like the greed for gold! Thirty-two years before Briscoe discovered gold, Wapello County had watched as vehicles of every description, carrying Forty-niners, passed through town on the way to Eddyville. There they crossed the river and headed west to the Mormon Trail of 1846, which would lead them to El Dorado in California.

There were so many gold seekers in 1849 that the original publishers of the *Ottumwa Courier*, J. H. D. Street and R. H. Warden, were in fear of Ottumwa becoming a ghost town before its roots were firmly implanted. The rush for gold caused the men to lament, "When will the ever restless, grasping desires – mania we should say— of our countryman for adventure become satisfied?....When will they be satisfied with the beautiful and productive land where their lot has been cast?"

An Agency merchant took to heart the old adage, "Make hay while the sun shines," and placed an advertisement in The Courier with the heading, "The Nearest and Best Road to California." At the time there was an endless parade to Council Bluffs through Agency from Jefferson County and points farther east of those full of "mania." The merchant offered pistols, Bowie knives, revolvers, boots, shoes, blankets, ready made clothing – all at a reduced price.

Typical of an advertisement was "Bound for California: Farm for Sale." It was placed by William F. Bay. Offering his 280 acre farm north of Dahlonega for sale at a "bargain" caused the following comments from Mr. Warden and Mr. Street on April 9, 1850: "While this California movement increases the price of grain and stock, it has forced into the market quite a number of good farms, which are offered at reduced prices. Now is the time for those who wish to make advantageous settlement in Iowa to buy."

Earlier, in the April 2, 1850 edition of *The Courier*, they wrote: "As we stand in our office door and see this mighty army of gold seekers steadily moving on impelled by magic . . . .a feeling of sadness comes over us as we reflect on the misery and suffering many of these adventurers will undergo . . . ."

Three decades later, when Mr. Briscoe announced that he had discovered gold in Wapello County one and a half miles from the mouth of Bear Creek, $40-an-acre ground shot up to $500 an acre, with one speculator paying $2,000 for a tract.

Much to his credit, the editor of *The Courier*, Major Hamilton, never believed there was gold in "them thar hills" southwest of Ottumwa, and discouraged the idea. At the time of this gold strike, prominent Ottumwa businessmen went "insane," so history books record, and it wasn't until later that a committee came to their senses and sent a specimen to Chicago, only to receive the disheartening verdict of "no gold – no silver."

Thus, the gold rush ended with a whimper, leaving the victims of the rush —Ottumwa businessmen — with empty pockets, and the profiteers — South Ottumwa farmers and landowners — with much deeper pockets by the selling of mineral rights or actual ground.

Mr. Briscoe left for the real gold fields of Montana, leaving behind what were most likely harsh feelings for South Ottumwa by north Ottumwa perpetuated by greed on both sides of the river.

Michael W. Lemberger

Indian Rock, on Bear Creek, not far from where J. O. Briscoe discovered "gold"

LATTER-DAY NOAH'S ARK

In 1903, *The Courier* announced that the Memorial Day Parade would be cancelled if the rains continued, and continue they did. As the fates would have it, instead of holding a parade, community leaders and interested citizens met at the Grand Opera House to assess what flooding was occurring in the wards of the city and where help was needed.

North and South Ottumwa were being hit by the flooding of the Des Moines River, which was breaking all previous records for high water. No lives were lost, but a horseback rider was nearly drowned on Church Street when he was swept from his horse. Both horse and rider were rescued from what was a portent of things to come

Lemberger collection

Church Street, in South Ottumwa, during the 1903 flood

when the Granddaddy of all floods swept across Ottumwa in 1947, which did result in loss of life.

As could be expected, the South Side, Central Addition, and the West End of Ottumwa were the hardest hit. A committee of South Ottumwa business men, which included lumber merchant John Wormhoudt, grain merchant John Weidenfeller, and cigar manufacturer and bicyclist Tom Pallister were aided in their efforts by Father Thomas O'Farrell, the priest of St. Patrick Church, in organizing an evacuation effort to the North Side with the help of oarsmen from the Ottumwa Boat Club and others.

The evacuees who could be induced to leave were taken to the south end of the Market Street Bridge, then walked over the bridge and down the Milwaukee tracks and taken to one of more than 20 private homes and public facilities to safety.

Monday morning, June 1, 1903, found 500 victims homeless in Central Addition with over 100 homes under water. To sell lots in that part of the city, Central Addition had been advertised as the "garden spot" of the community, but this garden spot was under water and always would be during high water periods. Though the West End was flooded first, with a levee giving way in part, the East End also succumbed with Hayne Street being flooded. Families there had taken the precaution of finding safety, but those at the foot of College Street would not move, and suffered great loss in family goods.

John Morrell & Co. was not surrounded by water, but overflow water entered several floors, creating havoc in the engine and firing rooms and rendering two boilers inoperable.

Dain Manufacturing (now John Deere Ottumwa Works) suffered little damage, but photographs show that inventory standing in their yard awaiting shipment was flooded. Businesses on Church and Main Streets were heavily damaged, with the foundations of several businesses on Church Street undermined by water. The section of the brick street nearest the Market Street Bridge was washed away by the fast, heavy current.

Grocery stores that could open, though flooded with several feet of water, allowed men on horseback to purchase enough undamaged flour for a week. There were no newspapers reports of the modern-day expected occurrence of looting.

FATHER WARD'S CALL

With the growth of South Ottumwa, which included not only Pickwick but Port Richmond, streets were named for those who were influential in the growth of this area, not the least of whom was Father Francis Ward

Father Ward, born and educated in Ireland, was ordained June 9, 1879, in Dubuque and sent to Ottumwa to serve the growing Roman Catholic community, which up until that time had been solely pastored by Father John Kreckel of St. Mary's parish. Father Kreckel's pastorate included not only Ottumwa, but Roman Catholics in surrounding communities.

Because members of this faith, including those on the south side of the river, found it difficult to travel the distance and cross the river for services, Father Ward

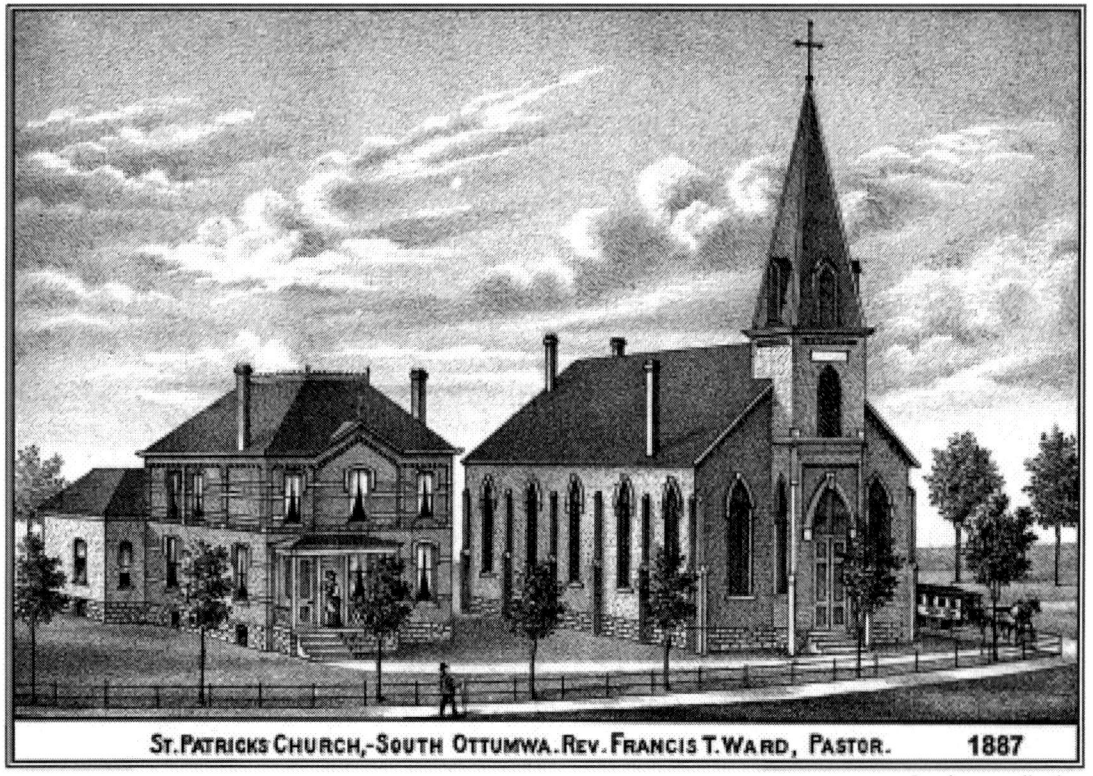

St. Patricks Church,-South Ottumwa. Rev. Francis T. Ward, Pastor. 1887

Lemberger collection

Fr. Francis Ward, the first priest to serve South Ottumwa

was an answer to their prayers.

Father Ward conducted services in homes, as well as the schoolhouses at Bear Creek, Elm Grove and Happy Hollow, from the time he arrived until the diocese purchased a lot from Dr. W. B. Smith. The cornerstone for the new church was placed in 1880, and St. Patrick's Church was completed in 1882. Dr. Smith subsequently donated two more lots on which were built a rectory in 1884 and eventually a school.

Lemberger collection

When dedicated on April 15, 1883, the building presented an imposing image at the corner of what was to become Church and Ward Streets.

Erected on a "firm foundation" of stone, the 40 by 80-foot brick structure gleamed with stained glass windows and a roof of slate. It wasn't until 1890, when Father Ward traveled to his homeland for a visit, that the original tower was replaced with a high spire incorporating a church bell, truly completing this parish home for the nearly 140 families it served.

Years after Father Ward was transferred to a parish in Iowa City, held in memory by only a few parishioners, the little parish church which he founded served its last mass in 1956. It was replaced by the present structure, with its first mass held August 4, 1957.

There are those who still remember "old St. Pat's," but for those who are too young, a statue of St. Mary from the original church holds a constant vigil in its memory on the street side of the current church. It honors Father Ward, reminding us that Father Ward and St. Patrick's Church are synonymous with South Ottumwa.

Days Gone By

MR. DIEHN and HIS BOXES

    Cigar manufacturing was a big industry for Ottumwa, getting its start in the early to mid 1880s. But most of the manufacturers, with a few exceptions, did not make their own boxes. A young man by the name of August Diehn came to Ottumwa June 1, 1890, when he purchased the Krabbenhoeft cigar box manufacturing company on Church Street.

    Mr. Diehn was born in Davenport in 1873, and learned the craft of cigar box making while an apprentice in his father's cigar box manufacturing company. He operated his wooden box-making business — Ottumwa Cigar Box — at 708-710-712 Church Street, where the name of the business can still faintly be seen on the side of the brick building. Ottumwa Cigar Box had little competition, and what there was posed no threat to its success. Diehn had one of Ottumwa's most successful businesses, employing twenty-five persons. He operated the Ottumwa Cigar Box company for exactly twenty-nine years, retiring June 1, 1929.

    It is little wonder that Ottumwa Cigar Box did such a thriving business, as Ottumwa was one of the leaders in the cigar-making industry in the state. The earliest brand of cigars in Ottumwa was the La Flor De Mayo, made by D. F. Morey.

    George Potter, a salesman for D. F. Morey beginning in 1884, founded his own company in 1899 with Logan McKee, naming it McKee and Potter. As with a number of the cigar-manufacturing businesses, this business relationship dissolved in 1917. Potter formed George Potter and Brother at 134 West Second Street, while McKee formed a company at 119 West Second Street with F. D. Marks, Jr., called McKee and Marks. Mr. Morey's cigar was later made under the company names of Stentz & Bohe; John T. Bohe & Co., and later W. A. Hendricks. The Graves Cigar Factory was in business for over thirty years and the Pallister Brothers for nearly thirty-eight years.

    The biggest name in Ottumwa's cigar-making industry was Julius Fecht, who came to Ottumwa as a cigar maker in 1874 and opened his business in 1884. Working sixteen hours a day, he built his business into one of the largest in the state with a five-story factory and warehouse which still stands at 302 West Main Street. He was the only manufacturer to be also a grower and importer of Havana tobacco, having a Cuban partner to facilitate his business.

Lemberger collection

August Diehn came to Ottumwa during its most exciting period, and while active in the business community's affairs, he served as president of the L.T. Crisman Co. and director of the Ottumwa Supply and Construction Co. Mr. Diehn died in 1948, but his stately home, built from the revenue of the sale of cigar boxes, still stands at 180 North Ward Street.

Thomas Quinn, while president of the Wapello County Historical Society, made a comprehensive study of the cigar manufacturing industry in Ottumwa and produced an unpublished work on which this article is based.

EDITH'S ROOM

When Edith Margurite Foster was born on February 4, 1889, she was number seven of ten children born to Thomas Dove (T. D.) Foster, who brought John Morrell & Co. to Ottumwa, and the third child for him and his second wife, Eliza Jane McClelland. T. D.'s first wife, Elizabeth, had died in 1879, leaving him with four children. It was six years later that he met Eliza Jane at a church function, and requesting that he might accompany her home, found she was the principal of Lincoln School, the school which his four children attended. The love bug struck and they were married in 1885, realizing a happy marriage that ended just short of thirty years later when T. D. succumbed to heart disease at the age of sixty-seven in July, 1915.

In Edith's memories of her life, audiotaped and transcribed for her family, she recalls a very full life with a very loving father in a home at 205 East Fifth Street – the corner of Fifth and Market. The architectural style of the house escaped her, but in her mind it struck her as "Early Standard Oil."

The house was remodeled in the early 1920s by Edith's sister, Ellen Foster Bell.

Lemberger collection

205 East Fifth Street, the home of Thomas Dove Foster

Sue Parrish

Ellen moved into the home with her mother after the death of her husband, Harold Bell, from cancer left her with two children, the youngest only five months old. The house stands today in the remodeled Tudor Style.

Edith could hardly wait for a room on the third floor to be furnished "in any way I please." At the age of twelve, she was able to move into one of the two bedrooms which, accompanied by the clothes-drying room and a large playroom papered in Mother Goose characters, occupied the top floor. Her room allowed her a spectacular view of the Des Moines River Valley.

Furnishing the room directly above her parents' room with a brass bed and bird's-eye maple dresser and desk, she was especially thrilled with the dressing table made for her by her fourteen-year-old brother, George, over which she hung a sheer organdy curtain over pink muslin. An ornate mirror was then hung over this girl's dream come true.

One night, believing that one had to suffer anguish for one's prayers to be heard, she decided to stay up all night on her knees "agonizing in prayer" beside her brass bed. Falling asleep and hitting the floor with a thud which awakened her, she got back on her knees to continue her agonizing. A deeply devout Christian, her father must have been amused when he was awakened by the thud above him and was told by Edith what had happened. T.D. assured her that God would hear her prayers just as easily with her lying in bed, as well as on her knees!

Another incident in her much-loved room brought her mother to investigate. Edith liked to awaken early to study instead of staying up at night. As it was grape jelly making season, she had placed a dish of stewed Concord grapes on her bedside table with her lamp, alarm clock and a school book. Awakening in the morning to the alarm clock, she knocked the lamp and the clock from the stand, as well as making a mess of her sheets with stewed grapes. When her mother arrived, Eliza knew exactly what to do with the grape-stained sheets.

Though raised in a home of privilege, those living at 205 East Fifth were not spared grief. Edith's younger brother, Robert, born with a congenital heart condition, died New Year's Day, 1905, followed by her married half sister, Mary Foster Hormel, eight months pregnant, of a heart attack on July 4, 1907, and, of course, her father in 1915. But the greatest grief of all for Edith was the death in 1921 of her three-year-old daughter, Jane, who died as a result of a fall from the second floor while trying to slide down the banister. Edith, home on a visit, had warned Jane, but to no avail. This occurred five months after the untimely death of her sister Ellen's husband, Harold Bell, proving, once again, that good monetary fortune cannot ward off life's circumstances shared by all.

Days Gone By

THE INVISIBLE WORKING WOMEN

The ratio of women to men within Ottumwa's labor force during the "Golden Age" will never be known, but women were the backbone of the cigar manufacturing industry here. Their counterparts in the highly-industrialized city of Lowell, Massachusetts predominated in that city's labor force. With Ottumwa's burgeoning industrial complex at the end of the 19th century, the city was touted as "The Lowell of the West."

A. G. Harrow, secretary of the Johnston Ruffler Co., which encompassed a block on Main Street at the foot of Wapello Street housing their subsidiary, the Ottumwa Iron Works, tells in his recollections that the company employed 525 persons during the peak years. "Persons" is the operative word; a photograph in the collection of the Wapello County Historical Society, taken during the 1890's of thirty-five Johnston Ruffler Co. employees, shows that twenty-five of these are women. Reports from primary source material state that the Johnston Ruffler Company employed five hundred men during its peak years between 1882 and 1892.

We have a romanticized idea of that time period —The Victorian Age — when society deemed factory work unacceptable for women and somehow immoral. So it does not occur to us that many of the laborers in these industrial complexes were women, even though we are well aware of the immigrant women and children trapped in the sweatshops of the New York City garment district.

A mass migration of Swedish immigrants to the Midwest occurred between 1880 and 1914, though slower migration began much earlier. Wapello County became the final destination for many of these immigrants; they sought out industrial communities for employment, because more Swedish immigrants lived in cities in their homeland than on farms. Most Swedish immigrants had a secondary education before arrival. They saved their salaries from these labor-intensive American jobs, enabling them to attend schools of higher learning or purchase their own businesses, which may have included farms. Goal-oriented immigrants cared little if they were shunned by their "betters" as they worked for the pot at the end of the rainbow.

Longdo collection

Workers at the Walter T. Hall Candy Company, on the steps of the factory at Third and Market Streets.

Suffice to say, not all of Sweden's young immigrant women, or immigrant women from other European countries, were domestics. Many were at the bottom rung at the foot of the hill in factories enabling their sisters to have work at the top of the hill, in the homes of the wealthy industrialists who owned the factories at the foot of the hill.

This is in memory of the forgotten women who were a major part of the industrial work force, for as we all know, at the bottom is the foundation.

Days Gone By

"A BRILLIANT SOCIETY EVENT"

The Ottumwa *Daily Democrat* reported on a dinner dance in 1893 with the headline "A Brilliant Society Event at the Ballingall Hotel on New Year's Night." It reported that "of all the social events of this holiday season perhaps none was of a higher character or proved more successful than the Royal Arcanum dance."

The Royal Arcanum Society was the first of many fraternal benefit societies in the United States, with members of the business community joining for life insurance coverage. It was founded in 1877 and is still in business today, providing life insurance, annuities and educational loans to its members from the society's Boston headquarters. Most early life insurance companies were bankrupt after a few years, but the first life insurance company, New York Life, founded in 1845 as the Nautilus Insurance Co. to provide insurance to slave owners for their human property, is one of the nation's largest insurance companies.

Longdo collection

Dining room of the Ballingall Hotel

Sue Parrish

Mrs. G. Frank Spry (Bernice Whipple Spry), a leader of Ottumwa society around the turn of the 20th century

Parrish collection

As the Ballingall Hotel was known all over the Midwest for its cuisine and hospitality, it is not surprising Ottumwans would choose to hold their special events in the Ballingall's 40- by 65-foot dining room. The *Daily Democrat* told its readers "the whole affair was one of elegance, and one (of) which the Royal Arcanum may justly feel proud." Menus of the Ballingall from that time period contain every kind of fish, meat and fowl as well as every condiment, fruit and dessert imaginable, shipped to Ottumwa's railroad hub from large markets everywhere.

Peter Ballingall spared no expense in building and maintaining his dream hotel. Following the railroad west from Chicago to Galesburg, Illinois and on to Keokuk, Bentonsport, Fairfield and Agency, this Scotsman – born in Glasgow and called "Pete" by his friends – set down his hotelier roots in Ottumwa in 1858. He first purchased the hotel owned and operated by Ottumwa pioneer, Tay Sinnamon. But finding this structure unsuitable for remodeling, Ballingall built the four-story Ballingall House in 1864. Through continued remodeling and construction it became the iconic Ballingall Hotel. The Ballingall House with its brick structure and mansard roof was one of two hotels Ballingall owned in Ottumwa. As he operated the Depot Hotel, several blocks east of the Ballingall, "Pete" also operated a stage line for nine years between Ottumwa and Bloomfield.

It is no accident with Ballingall's experience and reputation that "not only was Ottumwa's best society represented, but quite a number of the elite from surrounding cities participated" in this brilliant New Year's dinner and dance society event.

Days Gone By

A WORK FOR CARRIE NATION

Why Carrie Nation, the six-foot-tall member of the temperance movement, who looked and acted like a bulldog, did not run amuck with her hatchet here is a question Ottumwans might ask themselves. Maybe she was out of steam in 1908, when Ottumwa had a block named "Battle Row" on Market Street with seven saloons, and held the record for the number of saloons of any city in the state. Or maybe she left her message for Billy Sunday to make.

Even in 1851 when D. W. McKelvey came to Ottumwa with his family, he noted that this little hamlet of 275-300 people had twelve saloons offering whiskey for 50 cents a gallon. Being realistic, saloons and whiskey runners, beginning with Indian traders, were at the forefront of the westward movement with the certainty of a good livelihood.

Maybe Carrie felt her large 175-pound figure was no match for the roustabouts and railroaders who enjoyed refreshment at Stormy Jordan's Road to Hell saloon in the basement of Peter Ballingall's Depot Hotel on East Samantha Street. The population of this industrial mecca, with three breweries, may have been too much for her hatchet. Immigrants from Germany, including Bernhard Hofmann,* brought with them from their homelands the great secrets of beer brewing, opening breweries in Ottumwa to feed the thirst for German beer. These German brewmeisters, moving into the Midwest, built the foundation for the great American breweries of the future.

It was actually in the 1870s, and before Carrie Nation, that Ottumwa's most famous and wise saloon keeper, the abstaining Kinsey "Stormy" Jordan. moved his business from the basement of the Depot Hotel to South Market Street, opening as the Corn Exchange. He retired before the ratification of the 18th Amendment, which prohibited the sale of alcohol, would have put him out of business in 1919.

Longdo collection **Billy Sunday**

Sue Parrish

Carrie Nation

Longdo collection

Iowa's communities battled for prohibition on a limited scale with German brewmeisters from the latter part of the 19th century until Ottumwa's state senator, Edwin G. Moon, got his foot in the door with the passage of the Moon Law in 1909, which became effective March 1, 1910. At the time, this county seat held the dubious record for the number of saloons, with 43 saloons for a population of 18,000. The law prohibited Iowa from licensing more than one saloon per 1000 persons in a county.

As the west was being tamed, it was an interesting period during our history. Carrie Nation and Iowa-born former baseball player Rev. Billy Sunday, who did evangelize in Ottumwa from November 6 to December 16, 1908, gave their own brand of temperance messages. The hatchet-wielding "bulldog" dropped her hatchet as she headed for the Pearly Gates in 1911. William "Billy" Sunday followed November 6, 1935, two months after viewing a World Series game and one week after his last sermon.

*Bernhard Hofmann constructed the original Hofmann Building— an office building— on the southwest corner of Market and Second Streets. His son, Frank, became a pharmacist with his pharmacy business in this building. This original structure was consumed by fire on Easter Morning, 1940. It was replaced with the current Hofmann Building on this site.

Days Gone By

SON OF ZEUS

With buildings of wood-frame construction, every frontier community was vulnerable to the whims of Vulcan, Zeus's son -- the god of fire. Whether from overheated stoves, creosote in chimney flues, spontaneous combustion, sparks, or in many cases arson, it was not uncommon for communities to suffer major losses to business districts, and Ottumwa was no exception. Vulcan consumed eight buildings in Ottumwa's downtown on January 22, 1868. But that was just an appetizer, as nine months later on October 30 the entree was served, consuming twenty-two buildings — most of the main business district in the heart of town. It was a terrible loss for the community, as it was going through growing pains, and only $225,000 of the $400,000 loss was covered by insurance.

Smaller losses were frequently incurred over the years. The entire block on the north side of Main Street between Green and Jefferson went up in flames on March 1, 1877. One must remember that though business structures were susceptible, private homes were even more vulnerable. As the town became a larger railroad center, one of the causes of house fires was sparks from engines igniting roofs on homes located near the tracks. It must also be remembered that fighting fires in the early days was anything but a good time with wind direction a major factor, as it continues to be today.

Arson was suspected to be the cause of the J. D. Ladd & Co. pork packers plant fire on October 8, 1873. Twenty years later, in 1893, after John Morrell & Co. had purchased the plant from Ladd's, a fire broke out one evening at the plant as T. D. Foster, president of the North American operations of the company, was taking his wife and a daughter for a buggy ride in his one-seater. Excitement settled over the community as whistles and sirens went off. Mr. Foster hurriedly dropped his wife and daughter off at a nearby house and raced his buggy two miles to the plant, turning over his horse to someone and giving him instructions on the care of the lathered-up animal. T. D. was able to rescue the most important documents and files from his office before it burned. The plant was a total loss, which allowed for the construction of a new plant with the most up-to-date equipment in the meat packing industry at the time. The individual whom Foster had entrusted with his horse took advantage of the situation, giving people rides and destroying the horse for further use. T. D. was forced to retire the horse to his farm west of town.

On July 21, 1911 a fire – believed to have been caused by bare electrical wires – destroyed the furniture store of W. H. Cooper & Sons on the southwest corner of

Sue Parrish
Lemberger collection

Morrell fire, 1893

Court and Main Streets. It had the potential for becoming one of the biggest and costliest of fires to that date, but firewalls on each side of the building held, as firefighters poured streams of water onto the blaze from the roof of the building next door. A trolley repair wagon from the Railway and Light Co. was pulled up for firemen to stand on to fight more effectively.

The Easter morning fire on March 24, 1940, brought to an end one of Ottumwa's notable landmarks — the original Hofmann Building on the southwest corner of Second and Market Streets. Though a second Hofmann Building was constructed on the site, it didn't command the attention of the original which, when it was built, was the tallest building in Ottumwa.

Another notable fire the older generation will remember was an electrical fire which destroyed the Wapello County Tuberculosis Hospital on New Year's Eve, December 31, 1944, with the loss of one life, a patient, from smoke inhalation. The facility, which had been a summer retreat for T. D. Foster, named Sunnyslope, had been sold in 1917 to Wapello County by his family after his death in 1915.

There have been many other horrendous fires, including those with loss of life. Vulcan may not exist, but the destruction from fire is real.

Days Gone By

A FATEFUL FEBRUARY FIFTH

A beautiful Clara Rosen, daughter of Swedish immigrants and engaged to be married, left her family home at 1011 Locust Street at 6:25 p.m. on the cold evening of February 5, 1909 to walk alone to the home of her sister, Mrs. Gust Nelson on Dare Street. Clara's brother, Fred, had requested to escort her, but she refused his company, feeling secure enough to go alone.

Clara walked north on Cherry Street to Fourth Street and then west on Jefferson to Dare Street where, after she had walked less than 100 feet, the left side of her head was struck from behind, causing her to fall to the ground bleeding. The perpetrator carried her to an excavated basement nearby where the attack continued. The slight Ms. Rosen was no match for her assailant, and after a brief and feeble struggle, she died from a crushed skull.

When she failed to arrive at her sister's home, an intensive search by police and the community ensued. It wasn't until four o'clock the next morning when her brother Fred and his 24-year old friend, Otto A. Johnson, who would later retire from John Morrell & Co. as head cashier, located her body. It was such a shocking event for the young Mr. Johnson, whose family and Clara's were close friends and neighbors, that he never spoke of the event for the rest of his 94 years.

Her clothes were torn and disheveled, with one hand clutching the handle of her purse while her purse and its contents were missing. The other hand was bare, her engagement ring missing. Nearby was the eight-inch-square blood-covered rock used to bludgeon her to death. Her brooch, with a large stone missing, was also found.

Three weeks later her murderer was arrested, with elements involved in the crime as up-to-date as today's headlines. The perpetrator was found to be a former convict and alcoholic with a cocaine addiction, and of his guilt there was no doubt. He had shown the engagement ring to a friend, Mrs. Clutter, less than three hours after the crime, then removed the stone and sold it to Redman's pawn shop on February 16, throwing the mounting in the catch basin in the men's restroom in the Wabash Depot. The other items taken from Clara's body, including a bracelet and a string of gold beads, were found in the attic of his mother's home.

News story about the murder

The Ottumwa Girl Whose Brutal Murder John Junkin Confesses

CLARA ROSEN.

"Why?" is the question asked. In his confession, he admitted to drinking heavily the day the murder occurred, and said that when he encountered Clara at the corner of Jefferson and Gara Streets, he decided to rob her.

His pre-trial safety was of great concern, because the murderer, John Junkin, was a black man and the memory of a "lynching" of an innocent man which took place at the corner of Market and Main Streets in 1893 was still fresh in the minds of law enforcement. (In that case, a Swedish gentleman, who could not speak English, was accused of rape and later found not to be guilty, which didn't avail him much after he had already been hung!)

For safety's sake, Junkin was moved by train to jails all over southeastern Iowa to await trial. After authorities found the Sigourney jail unsafe, Junkin was pumped by handcar to Washington, and later to Burlington, where a huge rock was thrown through the train window, causing him to be removed to the baggage car. The train then proceeded to Ft. Madison where he was confined until his trial was held in Centerville.

With the preponderance of evidence, Junkin was found guilty and sentenced to death. He was hanged at the state penitentiary in Fort Madison on July 29, 1910, bringing to an end one of the most sorrowful and needless events in Ottumwa's history.

Days Gone By

IN CELEBRATION OF INDEPENDENCE DAY

There was a time when great bonfires, picnics, races of all kinds and parades were topped off by patriotic speeches given by politicians in town squares to celebrate our Declaration of Independence, July 4, 1776, as celebrated in Kirkville, Iowa on July 4, 1863. What a day it was! First there was the parade followed by the "tedious reading of the Declaration of Independence and the fiery speeches." The speeches dwelt on General Grant's siege of Vicksburg, and lasted so long that by the time they were finished, everyone was so hungry that a general scramble ensued to get to the dining tables, But the best was yet to come: A dispatch arrived announcing that Grant had taken Vicksburg! The sounds of the hoopla that followed can still be heard over the hills of Kirkville today, as never again would a July Fourth celebration end with such excitement.

In cohesive little hamlets across the nation, this holiday is still celebrated in the old-fashioned way, but it is now more often celebrated with a backyard barbecue among family and friends with the Stars and Stripes hanging intermittently up and down the avenues. The family canine, though, is still hiding under a bed, traumatized by the setting off of fireworks as in those days of yore.

Memories from childhood are crowded with holiday scenes, not the least of which is this glorious of all patriotic days. Each holiday captures its own ambience, and at any given moment, it can become the most significant. Such is the case held in the memory of Edith Foster, one of ten children of T. D. Foster, who recorded for her family in 1954 the happy events of "Fourth of July — Almost Any Year."

A picnic was planned days in advance with the family gathering for each to give input to where it should be held. Each child was allowed to bring a friend to the celebration, and the family servants were always included. Edith voted to travel to the south side as it was always exciting to ford the river in the large lorries borrowed from the John Morrell & Co. plant for the day, with the drivers a large part of the family picnic, too. Edith explained that the lorries had iron wheels, so the holiday-decorated lorries were filled with hay to ease the jolts going over the unpaved streets. The fording of the river was the big excitement of the day, which elicited shrieks for thoughts of the horror of being swept down the river. Edith relates they never used a bridge to cross the river, which leaves one to contemplate that their father may have deemed fording the river part of the great holiday excitement.

Sue Parrish

After finding a shady grove for the picnic, a level spot was located for the fifty gallon pail of iced lemonade to be placed for use throughout the day. And, as many of us look forward to it today, fried chicken was the fare, served with corn. The ears were boiled in a large caldron on the family's picnic spot over a fire built from wood the children had gathered. The ever-present July Fourth watermelon was served for dessert. As the adults relaxed in folding chairs the rest of the day, the children played hide-and-seek, ran races and played tag when not using the rope swing, which had been hung upon arrival at the chosen picnic spot.

One wonders with the number of active children in attendance, though several were older, how many scraped elbows, torn britches and bug bites occurred, as even the very wealthy are not immune to these events!

We do know that one picnic was marked by the "unholy use of the lemonade" to put out a grass fire, and the last of the July Fourth family picnics took place in 1914, when, ill from heart disease and too exhausted from the day's activities, T.D. Foster had to be transported home by automobile while the others took the usual lorries.

Mr. Foster, the most influential personage in Ottumwa, died a year later on July 20, 1915.

Lemberger collection
Thomas Dove (T. D.) Foster

Days Gone By

THE NORTH GREEN HOME

The Tisdale Apartments, on the southwest corner of Fourth and North Green Streets, is famous in the area for being the home of former President Richard M. Nixon and Mrs. Nixon for the seven months he was stationed at the Ottumwa Naval Air Station during World War II. But just across Fourth Street, on the west side of North Green — number 207 — is a house in which a famous Iowan from the past was born.

When we think of famous authors associated with Ottumwa, Edna Ferber comes to mind, but she was not born here and she spent a limited period of her childhood in Ottumwa. A contemporary of Ferber's, Honore McCue Willsie Morrow was born to Ottumwa attorney William McCue and his wife, Lilly, in 1880 in the house on Green Street. An author and the associate editor of the *Delineator*, a woman's magazine, she was a famous Iowan in her day.

Honore, a lover of history and of Abraham Lincoln, was one of the first to author the genre of well-documented historical novels She graduated from the University of Wisconsin with a history major and married Henry Willsie, a construction engineer. Moving to Arizona for his employment opened the door for Honore to research American life in the southwest, and her stories about the area were published in *Collier's* and *Harper's Weekly*.

After two years in Arizona, she and her husband moved to New York, where in 1914 she became the managing editor of the *Delineator*. She worked at the *Delineator* for five years, then turned to full-time writing. When she and her husband divorced in 1922, she had already begun a ten-year quest in becoming an authority on Abraham Lincoln, which resulted in her becoming an established author with her trilogy, *Great Captain,* on Lincoln. The three books were titled *Forever Free, With Malice Toward None* and *The Last Full Measure*.

The following year she married William Morrow, who founded the William Morrow Publishing Co. in 1926. His company became one of the largest book publishing companies in the United States. Honore completed numerous principal novels including *Yonder Sails the Mayflower, Mary Todd Lincoln, The Father of Little Women, The Life of Bronson Alcott,* and many more. *Black Daniel*, her 1933 biography of Daniel Webster, who was a friend of her grandfather, was completed after William Morrow's death in 1931.

Sue Parrish

This gifted author and mother of three moved to England after her husband's death, living in a 16th-century cottage where she completed her last work, *Demon Daughter*, in 1939. The book was based on her own tempestuous daughter, Felicia.

The movie *On to Oregon*, made in 1975, was based on her book, *Seven Alone*, the story of a family of children traveling the Oregon trail after their parents' deaths. The movie, directed by Earl Bellamy, starred Dewey Martin, Aldo Ray, and Anne Collins.

Honore died in 1940 as a result of the flu, while visiting her sister in New Haven, Connecticut. She is remembered in literary circles as one of the first to give readers well-documented historical romance novels, and some of her books are still being reprinted. Her birthplace at 207 North Green Street in Ottumwa is remembered by none.

Longdo collection

The house at 207 North Green Street, where Honore Willsie Morrow was born, is at right, marked with an X in this postcard view.

CIVIC LEADERS' DUPLEX

There are many civic leaders whose names have been lost to history but who have had a lasting impact on the community. Two of these men, Ottumwa businessmen G. Frank Spry and John Weidenfeller, with their wives, Bernice Whipple Spry and Sarah Ainley Weidenfeller, both couples childless, moved into the Federal-style duplex at 435 North Court Street in 1916. The two couples built the residence together, and each side was a mirror image of the other. The Weidenfellers lived in the south half and the Sprys in the north half, sharing a black and white ceramic tile foyer, a tile used also in their second-floor baths.

John Weidenfeller came to Ottumwa in 1888 from Mineral Point, Wisconsin to work in the clothing business. He later operated the grain mill on Ottumwa's south

The Spry/Weidenfeller duplex at 435 North Court Street

side. Wholesale and retail grain dealer, G. Frank Spry, who was employed by W. E. Jones & Co. with their grain company at 307-309-311 West Main Street and elevator at 101 Tisdale Avenue, crossed paths with Weidenfeller and they became friends.

Mr. Weidenfeller, a city alderman from 1902 to 1908 and a city commissioner in 1920 and 1921, also served as the city's parks chairman in 1921. During his term as parks chairman he authorized the purchase of property that became the south half of Riverside Park and purchased, named and was responsible for the early development of Memorial Park. John Weidenfeller was a charter and life member of the local Elks Club, No. 347, where he held all offices. He was also the secretary of the Ottumwa Commercial Club from 1906 to 1917, and while active in the Trinity Episcopal Church, acting as a trustee, he was secretary of the Ottumwa Country Club for twenty years. A bank manager for the Union Bank and Trust Co., he retired in 1948 after twenty-three years of service.

Frank Spry, having worked for Jones & Co. since 1892, came into the business as a partner in 1902. By 1916, with his brother John also a partner, the company was known as the Spry Bros. Grain Co., though for a short while it was the Spry-Slutz Grain Co.

A very active civic leader, Frank Spry was president of the board of the Ottumwa Hospital Association, president of the Ottumwa Chamber of Commerce, president of the Wapello Club, a leader in the First Presbyterian Church, member of Ottumwa Rotary Club, member of Ottumwa Country Club, vice-president of the board and member of the Elks Club.

Frank Spry slipped at the top of the staircase on the highly-polished hardwood floor in their home at 435 North Court Street, falling down the steps and breaking his neck. He lingered, critically injured, in the Ottumwa Hospital for nearly a week before passing away May 2, 1943 at the age of seventy-five. His widow, Bernice, grieved for him until her own death in 1964 at the age of ninety-six.

An interesting anecdote remains. In life, the Sprys shared a duplex with another family. In death they share a gravestone; they are buried on the south side of a stone in Ottumwa Cemetery while their nephew, Roy McCartney, and his family are interred on the north side of the stone.

Sarah Weidenfeller passed away in 1949, three years before her husband. With no nieces or nephews living nearby, the disconsolate Weidenfeller was included by the niece of Mrs. Spry in the niece's family's activities until Weidenfeller's incapacity and death in 1952.

Gone are the days when the grocers from grocery store row on South Court Street delivered groceries to 435 North Court and the other homes on what was then commonly called "silk stocking hill."

Days Gone By

NICKELS AND DIMES

From the advice of Benjamin Franklin's *Poor Richard's Almanac*, we learn that "A penny saved is a penny earned." Nothing reminds us of this advice more than the memory of the long-gone dime stores, the largest competitors in that field being S. S. Kresge Co. and the F. W. Woolworth Co. Both were located in the same block on the same side of Ottumwa's Main Street.

S. S. Kresge Co., on the southwest corner of Market and Main Streets, is fondly remembered as Kresge's on the Corner. The chain, started by Sebastian S. Kresge in 1899 in Detroit, Michigan, opened store number 93 in Ottumwa in 1915. His competitor, F. W. Woolworth, had opened his first five-and-ten-cent store in 1879 and by 1911 had 586 stores. In 1913 he built the tallest building in the world — the Woolworth Building — in New York City.

So down on the corner, what couldn't be had at the five-and-dime that was here for nearly seventy years? What a plethora of delights awaited customers upon entering the door. Everything the tidy homemaker needed to embellish herself and her home was proudly displayed, with many a future bride purchasing all of her homemaking needs at that corner.

The 2-for-50-cents at the jewelry counter, fondly called twofers, and the Tangelo lipstick bin were the favorites of teenage girls. The counter with the tasseled blue bottles of *Evening in Paris* was the favorite of young beaux. All kinds of toys and games abounded with a much larger display near Christmas with ideas for Santa. While there was never the selection the stores have today, a large selection was not expected, as we had not reached the age of consumption, but practically every need of the family was met from diapers and underwear to pots and pans.

With the health standards of today, one could suspect that the open candy bins harbored nearly every disease known to man, what with chirping canaries in cages, turtles and goldfish, all awaiting new homes, and humans with dirty hands and multiple sneezes. The candy bins sent their aromas wafting through the air, tempting every shopper with a few morsels before departing with their treasures. And if they were ever poisoned by these morsels, they never knew it.

The soda fountain or counter, with its swivel stools, is always associated with your favorite five and dime. Every meal was accounted for while pies, cakes, doughnuts and rolls could be had throughout the day. Not only a favorite spot for teens after school and on weekends, and those employed downtown, but many a footweary shopper, before catching the next bus home, stoked up on Coke, coffee or a fruit ade of choice.

Woolworth's "down the street" occupied a larger space and had more merchandise, but offered the same service to customers. The doors of both businesses were closed during the years of urban renewal, but their commercial influence was on the wane as their day had passed. Both underwent a number of years of reorganization and Kresge's became K-Mart, ultimately owned by Sears, while Woolworth's name has filtered down to become Foot Locker, Inc.

Not much can now be purchased with a nickel or a dime, but a single piece of paper!

Michael W. Lemberger

S.S. Kresge Co. occupied the southwest corner of the intersection of Market and Main Streets. The building was incorporated into the redevelopment of the block after urban renewal in the 1970s.

Days Gone By

ENGLISH TUDOR YEARS

Every home has a story, as does this home at 2442 North Court, which was built in the popular Tudor style of the 1920s and 1930s and was the first home to win the citywide Christmas decoration contest in the 1930s. What makes it special? It was built during the depression by an ordinary, hardworking couple who realized the American dream which existed in the hearts of their parents: His coming from Sweden and hers planted here through the westward migration during settlement years. They were typical of the middle-class couples who chose Ottumwa to raise a family, and they took advantage of the opportunities the city offered for a foundation toward that goal.

When completed in 1931, the brick story-and-a-half home with fireplace, slate roof, and formal English gardens had a spectacular view of the beautiful woodland property known as Seven Acres, the home of Dr. and Mrs. F. L. Nelson, which had originally been built in the 1890s as a retreat for the First Congregational Church.

Otto Axel Johnson and Moss I. Dorr were married June 14, 1911 in the home of her parents, after postponing their nuptials for five years until a certain amount of money had been saved to secure a good start. Otto was six feet, two inches tall with thick, coal black hair and Moss, a petite five feet two, was strawberry blond. Before marriage, both had graduated from Ottumwa Commercial College and were working toward their future with him in the office at John Morrell & Co., and she as the legal secretary for Ottumwa attorney John Webber. When Webber was elected to the Iowa State Senate, Moss accompanied him to Des Moines as his secretary.

The years rolled by and the couple built their first home in 1915 on the southeast corner of Iowa Avenue and Fourth Street. Children came along, as Otto worked his way up in the Morrell office, while their lives revolved around their children and the Main Street Methodist Episcopal Church. By the fall of 1929, with the onset of the Great Depression, Otto and Moss were busy making plans for their new home on North Court Road while, as members of the Main Street Methodist Church, they were raising money for the completion of their new church home, Wesley Methodist Episcopal Church.

Otto, one of eleven children, was able to call on help from several of his brothers, especially Joseph, who was an electrician and carpenter for John Morrell & Co., for completion of the home. A sister, Loula, cooked the meals as Moss painted the entire interior. It was a nephew, Russell Johnson, son of another brother and a landscape architect in Chicago, who designed the formal gardens, which included a fountain and

Parrish collection

The Johnson house at 2442 North Court

gold fish pond in separate areas, with a landscape feature foreign to us today: A special clothes-drying yard enclosed by tall poplar trees and hedge to hide the clothesline. Two other features included a tennis court for the family's three sons, and an outdoor fireplace, still in use, for many picnics for the large, extended family. Plum trees and a vegetable garden completed the landscaping, with a small stable at the end of a concrete driveway leading to the back of this acreage, with Otto having done all concrete work.

The Depression years saw two of the boys off to college, with a third to follow later. The Johnsons opened their four bedroom, two-and-a-half bath home to Moss's elderly parents, and during World War II, the Johnsons rented the first floor of their home to navy personnel stationed at the Ottumwa Naval Air Station, while the Nelson home across the street became the Officers' Club.

Otto retired from John Morrell & Co. as head cashier, and he and Moss purchased a farm in Highland Township, where they spent their retirement years. When Moss left 2442 North Court Road, now the home of Mr. & Mrs. Robert Johnson who are no relation to Otto and Moss, she caused no small stir when the buyers realized she had taken her plantings and kitchen cabinets with her, turning the situation into a real estate agent's nightmare!

Days Gone By

12,618 PANES OF GLASS

Beginning in June, 1935, eleven years after the million-dollar Ottumwa High School was completed, engineer Joe Barn oversaw summer maintenance. His regular staff, as well as those added for the extra summer work, brought the custodial force to fifteen during the three-month summer break before resumption of classes in September. School custodial work is a year-round proposition, and in that summer of 1935, Mr. Bain and his staff labored the entire summer in maintenance and repair work on one of the state's most progressive educational facilities and the architectural gem of Ottumwa.

Work began with all of the woodwork and furniture throughout the structure being washed and polished. This all had to be dusted again before the first day of school after the most tedious task of cleaning the 701 outside windows, which included 12,618 window panes which had to be washed on both sides. (This chore would have rendered a number of sore arms, hands and fingers after having completed the washing of those 25,236 pieces of glass, to be added to the stiff neck from having cleaned 969 lights within the classrooms and corridors beforehand.)

All air ducts to the four floors of rooms were cleaned, which included the cleaning and conditioning of 53 electrical motors. (The school was built with an air conditioning system.) Painting included the following: "the lower part of all four floors, the ceilings of two corridors on two floors, shower room and toilets, the floors in the auditorium, where 1,350 persons can be seated, six classrooms, the kitchen and the cafeteria. A special preparation has been spread on the gymnasium floor so that it is conditioned thoroughly for the coming sports seasons."

If that wasn't enough, all of the brick work was repointed, the roof coped and firewalls repaired, while the windows in six rooms were weather stripped; a platform built on the auditorium stage to store scenery; a new bulletin board built for the art room; "a new door hung on the boiler room and a canopy for carrying of gasses from the fires was constructed over the front and top of two boilers. Two stokers were repaired. At Schaefer Field the wooden bleachers got a coat of paint."

Are you worn out yet? Well, "the checking of 290 radiators, 68 telephones, 60 clocks, 9 bells and 125 thermostats" took place and "two boiler feed-water meters, which will assist in checking the efficiency as well as cost of operating the boilers" were installed.

Now are you done in? Remember, everything in this nearly block long structure has to be dusted again before the first eager student arrives, and the school swimming pool has to be filled with 50,000 gallons of water!

That is what went on in the summer of 1935 at Ottumwa High School, and now, more than seventy years later, this beautiful piece of architecture has seen the construction of new front steps. Hopefully, these new steps will last another eighty years.

Lemberger collection

Ottumwa High School, during the 1940s

Days Gone By

THE EVIL WITHIN

Evil, which carried secrets, manifested itself in 1860 and 1939 with the deaths of two men: one by accident; the other by murder. The evil within was greed in both instances.

Greed found its opportunity in Eddyville in 1860 when Jonathan Maxon drowned in the Des Moines River. A witness on the riverbank, Ben Slemmons, assumed Maxon had been sucked under by quicksand, and as the "best diver and swimmer" on the river was Eddyville physician Dr. Buck, he was immediately summoned to join the search party. After diving in the area where Maxon went down, Buck reported that he could find no body and the search team should begin to seine the river below the site of the disappearance, as the current had probably carried the body downstream. The searchers found no body to retrieve, and Jonathan Maxon was left to rest in a watery grave.

In 1907 the truth finally emerged concerning the disappearance of Mr. Maxon, when Thomas Kale came forward to help Mrs. Maxon receive a pension due her upon the death of her second husband. Having to prove that her first husband, Jonathan Maxon, was deceased before she could collect the pension benefits from her second husband, Thomas Kale came forward and swore before a notary public that Dr. Buck had stolen the body of Mr. Maxon, enlisting the help of Dr. Buck's friend, Charles Lutz, in retrieving the body from the river.

Kale testified that he had caught a fish hook in his finger and in trying to locate Dr. Buck to remove it, noting the back door of the doctor's office was ajar, peering in, he saw the incomprehensible sight of the good doctor dissecting the body of Jonathan Maxon! Kale's fishhook was removed by Dr. Buck, after Kale swore he would never reveal the doctor's secret.

What was Dr. Buck's reason for this hideous misadventure? He needed a skeleton for his office, and instead of spending the money to purchase one through mail order, he used what became available. By the time the nefarious deed came to light, Dr. Buck had been deceased thirty years.

Seventy-nine years later on the ground floor of Ottumwa's tallest building—the Ennis Building— on the city's busiest corner at five minutes after twelve o'clock noon, 22-year old Arthur "Henry" Geifman was found in his shoe store by his assistant, Edward Hawks, lying behind the empty cash register with a bullet wound

The Professional (or Ennis) Building, where Arthur Geifman was murdered in 1939

Lemberger collection

from a .35 caliber weapon to the right side of his head.

A victim of greed in its worst form, Henry died shortly after being transported to the Ottumwa Hospital, less than a mile away.

A likely perpetrator was investigated on a tip, and Clair Swank, an unemployed convict from Kirkville, Mo. was arrested. Though he protested his innocence, the most damaging witness was the man Swank was rooming with at 501 N. Iowa Avenue: William Walker, a painter and known prevaricator.

Though Swank was found guilty, being convicted on purely circumstantial evidence, he was spared the death penalty. His attorney, Charles C. Ayres, Jr., believed the trial unjust, with the judge denying every motion open to the defense. The only conclusive evidence came from the F.B.I. in their determination it was Swank's weapon which killed Geifman.

Today, through forensics, Swank would not have been convicted. It was fourteen years later, while on his deathbed, that Walker confessed to having stolen Swank's gun and killed Geifman as he was robbing Geifman's shoe store. Swank, in reality, *was* sentenced to death, because when he was told of the admission of guilt by Walker, and his impending release from prison, the shock was too great, and he fell over dead – the victim of a heart attack.

THE DAYS OF THANKSGIVING

Not so long ago, the Christmas tree and decorations did not appear until Santa lit Rudolph's nose in preparation for his flight around the world. The Friday after Thanksgiving hasn't always been a time for shopping lunacy, seeing who could become the most rude, ridiculous and insane American. And Thanksgiving Day was not spent voraciously reading merchants' advertising, while plotting and planning the Christmas shopping spree for the next day, as department store chains readied for those wake-up calls to customers so that frantic buyers wouldn't miss the 5 a.m. opening.

Lemberger collection

Christmas decorations and shoppers at the intersection of East Second and Market Streets in 1941. Hotel Ottumwa is in the background.

Sue Parrish

In fact, on the day after Thanksgiving, Dad got up and went to work as usual, while Mom stayed home boiling the turkey carcass, freezing or preparing leftovers for another go-round, thinking of the weekend ahead, leaving the minors still pondering Squanto and being thankful they weren't pilgrims. Those minors would return to school; relate the events of the Thanksgiving Holiday; help the teacher take down the cut-out decorations of those dressed in black with buckled shoes and blunderbusses, then get back to reading, writing and arithmetic. The only hint of Christmas was the fruitcake aging in the refrigerator.

Thanksgiving Day, and those directly preceding and following, were the times to ponder for what we were truly grateful, while allowing our feasting to settle. Then and only then, did the aroma of evergreen boughs begin to waft through the crisp air, giving us the wake-up call of things to come.

It was about two weeks before that magical day of Christmas, when school and church program rehearsals got under way, while Market and Main Streets was abustle with Salvation Army bell ringers, as over a public address system we heard the Crooner singing *White Christmas* or Gene Autry telling us the tale of the red-nosed reindeer.

We wondered if there was to be a white Christmas, if we weren't already trudging through crunch underneath with cold noses and toes, carrying packages that consisted of one "special gift" for those on our list, feeling as if our gloved fingers had frozen to our clutched parcels.

What a relief to be welcomed by the blast of warm air as we entered another festive store dressed in the traditional red and green, realizing our fingers were coming alive. We were faced with one of two things as we left the latest plethora of holiday delight: We had either become too warm with our wool sweaters and heavy coats, and anxiously anticipated relief which was sure to come, or we dreaded the unrelenting blast of a Canadian Clipper from the North Pole.

Whatever was to come, we were ready with our red, green and white tissue paper and Christmas stickers, instead of Scotch tape, with which to wrap our carefully-chosen treasures to give. We munched on ribbon candy, wondering which one of our stockings we should choose for an elf to fill with an orange and walnuts.

Christmas stickers, ribbon candy, everyday stockings filled with an orange and walnuts topped by a candy cane, rest only in our memories with the Salvation Army kettle at Market and Main.

Days Gone By

MONDAY MORNINGS

Purchasing a restaurant on April Fool's Day was a portent of things to come... as if their lack of experience wasn't enough portent, when Vernel Toemmes left his position as superintendent of the receiving department at John Deere & Co., and his sister, Sabella Toemmes Harness, left hers as a secretary for the same company and entered into the most difficult of businesses: the restaurant business. They purchased Kelly's Café at 221 East Main Street in 1947, believing anyone could operate a restaurant: All you need is spunk, and they both had plenty of that. Vernell did not know how to cook, and Sabella did not know how to wait tables.

Sabella tells of her experiences in her reminiscence, *Fry Two,* relating when they purchased Kelly's, it was run by a manager and served 400 customers per day. Sabella and Vernell decided the manager wasn't doing anything but making decisions, and they could do that very well. They fired the manager as well as the cashier, who had been there 40 years and "knew every restaurant worker in town." Vernell became the manager and Sabella the cashier. They started their first day off not knowing how to open the cash register as "there were two keys and lots of buttons and gadgets." They pushed buttons until they got it to ring up something and Sabella took money out of her pocket to balance the tape at the end of the day. To top off this first day, the 2 p.m. cook did not show up so Vernell had his "baptism by fire."

Every morning is a Monday morning in the restaurant business, especially if you have a breakfast waitress who faints under stress. With a counter lined with customers, down she went. Those reading a newspaper had no idea their waitress had entered another world, and those who did were annoyed. The rubbing of hands and a cold towel did no good, so placing a clean towel under her head, Sabella took the guest check book from the slumbering waitress and pulled the legs of the sleeping beauty behind the counter so they could not be seen. Sabella proceeded with the task at hand, having to repeatedly step over the body. By this time the cook was out of sorts, banging with his spatula for assistance, while his ledge filled with orders. After the breakfast rush, the sleeping beauty opened her eyes, roused up and took her place

The interior of the Wapello Restaurant at 221 East Main, which later became Kelly's Cafe.

Longdo collection

behind the counter. Short of tearing off her apron and running out the door, this proved to be a good way to escape.

Relating the story of the drunk with a "happy smile on his face, and dull glazed eyes," Sabella tells of him placing three fried chicken orders to go, then promptly entering the men's restroom, locking the door and not coming out. Nothing roused the drunk, and after deciding he was asleep or dead, they told customers the restroom was out of order and waited until the restaurant had closed. Then they forced the door open, splintering the doorjamb. They found the drunk sound asleep on the floor, leaning against the wall. "S' matter, s'matter? Lemme alone" was all he could say.

Days Gone By

SWOOSH AND SOOT

Christmas Eve of 1948 became a Christmas Eve that Sabella Toemmes Harness and her brother, Vernel Toemmes, would never forget, as that was the Christmas Eve that they had a "hot time" in Kelly's Café at 221 East Main Street.

It was a crisp, cold day before Christmas with brilliant sunshine as Sabella finished her Christmas shopping and headed east on Main Street to the café she owned with her brother. As she proceeded down the street, arms piled high with packages, a bright red fire truck clanged by "all shiny and red it reminded me of a musical comedy scene," she said. "If they had broken into chorus it would not have surprised me at all, but they didn't. They clanged to a stop right in front of Kelly's Café!"

Sabella, anchoring her topmost package with her chin, took off on a run, hat bouncing askew. She pushed her way through the customers streaming out the front door, as firemen and hoses went in. She found her brother in the kitchen standing atop a meat block frantically spraying the ceiling with a fire extinguisher. The flames were swooshing across the ceiling and up a fire exhaust chimney, but it was not long before the firemen brought an end to the terrifying event, leaving the kitchen a muck-filled, dripping and steaming mess of soot, plaster and food, including fifteen pies, under a layer of goop.

There was little smoke damage to the rest of the building, with damage confined to the kitchen. This prompted the female insurance adjuster, who had been summoned, to graciously state over coffee and pie from the dining room, that it was "the much nicest fire she had ever visited."

After finding the coal-fueled stove would not draw, belching smoke back into the kitchen and hindering the cleanup process, a hesitant furnace expert arrived. As the "expert" began work, kitchen clean up also began: Tables and shelves were scrubbed along with the stove, grill, dishwasher, meat grinder and all dishes, glassware, pots and pans. After the last bit of fallen plaster, soot and grime had been shoveled out, it was 8 p.m., and with relief, Sabella realized she would be in form to wrap her packages and begin preparations for the first family dinner she and her husband, Lynn, were to host.

With everything in order, it was decided to fire up the stove to make certain it was ready for business when they reopened the day after Christmas. Lo and behold there

Anderson collection

This early view of Main Street shows the Kelly's Cafe sign midway down the block. to the right of the streetcar.

was a loud swoosh as soot billowed into the kitchen, recoating the entire area with the very familiar black grime and causing the furnace expert to exclaim, "This is the ... Christmas Eve I ever spent. I wish I had stayed away." With this the whole process began again.

Finally, at 3 a.m. Christmas morning, with shaking hands and thumping head, turkey slowly roasting in the oven, table set and packages wrapped, Sabella crawled into bed for a few hours' sleep before hosting her first family Christmas dinner as Mrs. Lynn Harness.

Days Gone By

AN IGNOBLE END

When Joseph Leighton became the Wapello County Treasurer in 1846, an office which also included the recorder's position, there were only eighteen houses in Ottumwa in a still sparsely populated county. But by the end of the century, when Mr. Leighton's wife Mary and daughter Abby were residing in a brick house at 118 North Jefferson – "a cozy home" with servants' quarters in the basement – Ottumwa and the county had hit boom times with stately homes throughout the city as well as the county. Mr. Leighton's son, Alvin, better known as A.C., became a very successful buyer and trader in real estate.

In 1870, twelve years after Joseph Leighton's death, A.C. sold 118 North Jefferson to his sister, Mary Emily, who had married Walter B. Jordan of the firm Leighton and Jordan, a mercantile business. Mary Emily deeded the property over to her widowed mother, Mary, in 1886, when Mary Emily and Walter moved to Minneapolis. Soon after, the elder Mrs. Leighton was sharing her home with her widowed daughter, Abby Jordan, who had married another of the twelve Jordan siblings (the brother of Mary Emily's husband). It was in this home in 1891 when Abby, assisted by her mother, entertained the ladies of society to a "delicate lunch" served in the dining room with white carnations as the foundation for a centerpiece with chrysanthemums scattered about, tied with ribbons in true Victorian fashion. The afternoon was spent playing drive whist, needing seven tables to accommodate the guests. Of course, suitable prizes, also in Victorian fashion, were given to the winners with Mrs. Arthur Gephardt, as first place winner, receiving a silver salt and pepper dish in a satin-lined case.

The years rolled by and the stately homes of the Bonnifields and the Bonhams, across from the Leighton-Jordan home, disappeared, giving way to commercial endeavors.

Then, nearly one hundred years after Abby's party, on a warm, sunny first day of spring – March 20, 1990 – the FBI descended on what had once been a stately home of mid-Victorian architecture and began a spring housecleaning by arresting the most prolific book thief in American history: Stephen Blumberg.

Blumberg had raped the house of all vestiges of architectural ornamentation from the interior, building shelves throughout the home from floor to ceiling where he housed 20,000 rare books and 10,000 rare manuscripts stolen from libraries across the United States.

There was a Judas in Blumberg's midst: He was sold out to the FBI for $56,000 by a close friend and associate who was living with him. The friend and informant, Kenneth Rhodes, rode around Ottumwa on a motorcycle with a red bandana flying out of his left hip pocket, and was as clean as the eccentric Blumberg was dirty.

The home at 118 North Jefferson Street died a slow death. It passed from being the genteel home of one of Ottumwa's first families in a noted, well-landscaped neighborhood, to being a filthy shell stripped of all its grandeur. It was razed by the father of Stephen Blumberg, after he failed to sell the dirty shell, whose ignoble end had already come.

Michael W. Lemberger

Moving vans hired by the FBI load up rare books which had been stolen by Stephen Blumberg and stored in the house at 118 North Jefferson (center).

EPILOGUE

There are as many stories as there are people who have walked the streets and the prairies of Wapello County. Change is imperceptible until viewed from a distance, and we must remember that the good old days are as close to us as yesterday, as life glides by on the swiftest of rivers leaving memories — the vignettes of our history posted in the scrapbook of time through the eyes of our soul.

-- Sue Parrish
October 24, 2007

Bibliography / Sources

Wapello County Historical Museum -- Archives of letters, scrapbooks and newspapers.

Wapello County Genealogical Society -- Archives of obituary records.

Evans, Capt. S.B., *History of Wapello County, Iowa, and Representative Citizens.* Biographical Publishing Co., Chicago, Ill. 1901.

The History of Wapello County. Western Historical Co., Chicago, Ill. 1878.

Meager, Glenn B. and Harry B. Munsell, *Ottumwa: Yesterday and Today.* Ottumwa Stamp Works Press, Ottumwa, Iowa. 1923.

Ottumwa *Courier*. Annual Trade Review. Ottumwa, Iowa, February, 1893.

Especially valuable for its primary source material were all sections of *The Ottumwa Daily Courier*'s August, 1923 Diamond Jubilee special edition.

Portrait and Biographical Album of Wapello County. Chicago, Ill. Chapman Brothers. 1887.

Quinn, Thomas, *Manuscript history of cigar box manufacture in Ottumwa, Iowa.* Unpublished.

Waterman, Harrison L., Supervising Editor. *History of Wapello County, Iowa.* Vol.1&2 Chicago, Ill. The S.L. Clarke Publishing Co. 1914.

Personal collection of family records and other ephemera, in the possession of the author.

Richard and Sue Parrish

About the Author

Sue Parrish's love of history began when she was a small child and her grandmother read to her a child's version of the life of Abraham Lincoln. She grew up on a farm in Dahlonega Township and attended the one room Dahlonega Dist. No. 1 school during the time Dahlonega was really in the country; when the dirt roads became knee deep ruts with the springtime rains, and the telephone connection was on a party line with over forty families.

She spent many hours reading in the woods on the farm where it was not hard for the imagination to be drawn to the tales of Daniel Boone and other frontiersmen and pioneers as they followed trails west.

Now retired, for sixteen years Sue was the registrar/coordinator—director—for the Wapello County Historical Society's museum. She writes a weekly historic interest article for the Ottumwa *Courier,* and can never leave a bookstore without something in hand. She spends her time between Ottumwa and Grinnell, Iowa where her daughter and family live.

Sue has a bachelor of arts degree with a history major and an English minor.

**Other books
from PBL Limited**

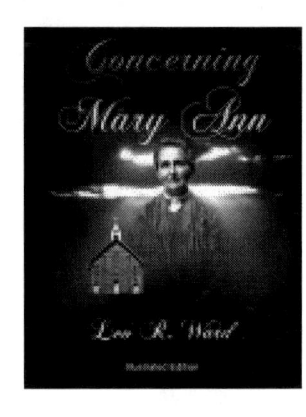

Focus on Photos $24.99
St. Patrick's Georgetown $24.99
Concerning Mary Ann $26.99
Meet Me At the Fair $19.99
"Come, Let Us Journey" $19.99
Pilgrimage $19.99
St. Joseph Hospital $19.99
Ottumwa $19.99
Ottumwa Postcards $19.99
Inklings $19.99
A Richer Dust Concealed $13.99
The Narrow Gate $19.99
Days Gone By $19.99
Coming Up Dry $19.99

*Visit www.pbllimited.com
to view other titles.*

Please add 7 percent sales tax (Iowa residents) and $4.00 per order for mailing in the United States. Send check or money order to PBL Limited, P.O. Box 935, Ottumwa IA 52501-0935.